Addi
Overseas
Business
Letters

Addressing Overseas Business Letters

by

Derek Allen

W. Foulsham & Co. Ltd.
London • New York • Toronto • Cape Town • Sydney

W. Foulsham & Company Limited
Yeovil Road, Slough, Berkshire, SL1 4JH

ISBN 0–572–01421–X

Copyright © 1988 Derek Allen

All rights reserved.
The Copyright Act (1956) prohibits (subject to certain
very limited exceptions) the making of copies of any
copyright work or of a substantial part of such a work,
including the making of copies by photocopying or
similar process. Written permission to make a copy
or copies must therefore normally be obtained from the
publisher in advance. It is advisable also to consult the
publisher if in any doubt as to the legality of any
copying which is to be undertaken.

Printed in Great Britain at
St. Edmundsbury Press,
Bury St. Edmunds.

CONTENTS

Introduction	6
The World – Suggested Business Languages	7
Commercial 'Territories' and their Parent Countries	15
Business Letters to European Countries	16
Austria	18
Belgium (French speaking)	20
Belgium (Flemish speaking)	22
Cyprus	24
Denmark	26
Finland (Finnish speaking)	28
Finland (Swedish speaking)	30
France	32
West Germany (Federal Republic of Germany)	34
Gibraltar	36
Greece	38
Iceland	40
Italy	42
Liechtenstein	44
Luxembourg (French speaking)	46
Luxembourg (German speaking)	48
Malta	50
The Netherlands	52
Norway	54
Portugal	56
Spain	58
Sweden	60
Switzerland (French speaking)	62
Switzerland (German speaking)	64
Switzerland (Italian speaking)	66
Turkey	68
Business Letters to Eastern European Countries	70
Albania	70
Bulgaria	72
Czechoslovakia (Czech speaking)	74
Czechoslovakia (Slovak speaking)	76
East Germany (German Democratic Republic)	78
Hungary	80
Poland	82
Romania	84
USSR	86
Yugoslavia	88
Guidelines for Letters to Various Important Trading Nations	90
Arab Recipients	90
Chinese Recipients	92
Japanese Recipients	92
Malaysia, Singapore and Brunei Recipients	93
Burmese Recipients	94
Thai Recipients	94

INTRODUCTION

This book gives advice on the writing of business letters abroad. It lists for practically every country in the world the language(s) used or acceptable for business purposes. There is also guidance on the correct language to use for the various territories (as opposed to countries) which are likely to figure in business and commercial correspondence. For example The Faroes and Greenland will follow the suggested business language of their parent country, Denmark.

For letters to Europe, the preferred language is the national language of the recipient, and for each country advice is given on addressing the envelope, including the title and name of the recipient, and the address itself, adopting the custom of the country in regard to the order and form used. The opening salutation and closing phrase in the letter is also given, using the national language of the recipient.

If the writer is obliged to use English, then at least the envelope should be correctly addressed, including the title to be used with the name. Although written in English, the letter can often take into account, in the salutation, the title to which the recipient is accustomed, in place of the English Mr, Mrs or Miss. This requires a judgment on behalf of the writer as to what is likely to be most acceptable to the recipient. For example, if a businessman in England receives a letter from Germany written in German, which salutation is preferable—'Sehr geehrter Herr Surname' or 'Sehr geehrter Mr Surname'?

The guidance on letter writing to Eastern Europe also contains some advice on the Organisations and Trade Departments to approach for doing business.

The book includes general guidelines for specific countries throughout the world where special approaches and forms of address are needed, for example the People's Republic of China, and the Arab world.

For business correspondents, problems sometimes arise with the typing of letters, for example to Bulgarian, Greek or Soviet Russian recipients, because of the different alphabet employed. As a general guideline, whilst letters in English are often understood, trade literature must always be in the national language, and type, both inside and outside Europe.

THE WORLD

Suggested business languages

The list which follows gives the principal countries throughout the world with the status or title of each, the capital city and the suggested business language(s) to use when writing. After the language(s) stated, the alternative (unless already given) is English.

Country	Status or title	Capital (English spelling in brackets to aid recognition)	Suggested business language(s)
Afghanistan	Democratic Republic	Kabul	Russian, English
Albania	People's Socialist Republic	Tiranë (Tirana)	Albanian
Algeria	Democratic and Popular Republic	Alger (Algiers)	French, Arabic
Andorra	Co-principality under French/Spanish sovereignty	Andorra la Vella	French, Spanish
Angola	People's Republic	Luanda	Portuguese
Antigua and Barbuda	Independent	St John's	English
Argentina	Republic	Buenos Aires	Spanish
Australia	Commonwealth Nation	Canberra	English
Austria	Republic	Wien (Vienna)	German
Bahamas	Commonwealth Nation	Nassau	English
Bahrain	Sheikhdom	Manama	English, Arabic
Bangladesh	People's Republic, Commonwealth Nation	Dacca	English
Barbados	Commonwealth Nation	Bridgetown	English
Belgium	Kingdom	Bruxelles (Brussels)	French, Dutch

7

Belize	Commonwealth Nation	Belmopan	English, Spanish
Benin	People's Republic	Porto Novo	French
Bhutan	Kingdom	Thimphu	English
Bolivia	Republic	La Paz	Spanish
Botswana	Republic, Commonwealth Nation	Gaborone	English
Brazil	Federative Republic	Brásilia	Portuguese
Brunei	Independent State	Bandar Seri Begawan	English
Bulgaria	People's Republic	Sofiya (Sofia)	Bulgarian
Burkina Faso (was Upper Volta)	Republic	Ouagadougou	French
Burma	Socialist Republic of the Union of Burma	Rangoon	English
Burundi	Republic	Bujumbura	French
Cambodia	Democratic Kampuchea	Phnom Penh	French
Cameroon	United Republic	Yaoundé	French English
Canada	Commonwealth Nation	Ottawa	English, French
Cape Verde	Republic	Praia	Portuguese
Central African Republic	Republic	Bangui	French
Chad	Republic	N'Djaména	French, Arabic
Chile	Republic	Santiago	Spanish
China	People's Republic	Beijing (Peking)	English, Mandarin
Colombia	Republic	Bogotá	Spanish
Comoros	Federal and Islamic Republic	Moroni	French, Arabic
Congo	People's Republic	Brazzaville	French
Costa Rica	Republic	San José	Spanish
Cuba	Republic	Habana (Havana)	Spanish
Cyprus	Republic, Commonwealth Nation	Nicosia	English
Czechoslovakia	Federal Socialist Republic	Praha (Prague)	Czech, Slovak
Denmark	Kingdom	København (Copenhagen)	Danish

Djibouti	Republic	Djibouti	French, Arabic
Dominica	Commonwealth Nation	Roseau	English, French
Dominican Republic	Republic	Santo Domingo	Spanish
Ecuador	Republic	Quito	Spanish
Egypt	Arab Republic	Cairo	English, Arabic
El Salvador	Republic	San Salvador	Spanish
Equatorial Guinea	Republic	Malabo	Spanish
Ethiopia	Socialist Republic	Addis Ababa	English, Arabic
Fiji	Commonwealth Nation	Suva	English
Finland	Republic	Helsinki	Finnish, Swedish
France	Republic	Paris	French
Gabon	Republic	Libreville	French
Gambia, The	Republic, Commonwealth Nation	Banjul	English
Germany, East	German Democratic Republic	Berlin (East)	German
Germany, West	Federal Republic of Germany	Bonn	German
Ghana	Republic, Commonwealth Nation	Accra	English
Gibraltar	British Semi-Colonial Rule	Gibraltar	English, Spanish
Greece	The Hellenic Republic	Athínai (Athens)	Greek
Grenada	Commonwealth Nation	St George's	English
Guatemala	Republic	Guatemala City	Spanish
Guinea	Republic	Conakry	French
Guinea-Bissau	Republic	Bissau	Portuguese
Guyana	Co-operative Republic, Commonwealth Nation	Georgetown	English
Haiti	Republic	Port-au-Prince	French
Honduras	Republic	Tegucigalpa	Spanish
Hong Kong	British Colonial Rule	Victoria	English, Cantonese
Hungary	People's Republic	Budapest	Hungarian

Iceland	Republic	Reykjavik	Icelandic
India	Republic and Union of States, Commonwealth Nation	New Delhi	English
Indonesia	Republic	Jakarta	English
Iran	Islamic Republic	Tehrán	English, French
Iraq	Republic	Baghdad	English, Arabic
Irish Republic	The Republic of Ireland	Dublin	English, Irish
Israel	The State of Israel Republic	Jerusalem	English
Italy	Republic	Roma (Rome)	Italian
Ivory Coast	Republic	Abidjan	French
Jamaica	Commonwealth Nation	Kingston	English
Japan	Democratic State with Emperor	Tōkyō (Tokyo)	English, Japanese
Jordon	Hashemite Kingdom	Amman	English, Arabic
Kenya	Republic, Commonwealth Nation	Nairobi	English
Kiribati	Republic, Commonwealth Nation	Tarawa	English
Korea, North	Democratic People's Republic of Korea	Pyŏngyang	English
Korea, South	Republic of Korea	Sŏul (Seoul)	English
Kuwait	Sovereign State	Kuwait	English, Arabic
Laos	Lao People's Democratic Republic	Vientiane	French
Lebanon	Republic	Beirūt	English, Arabic
Lesotho	Kingdom, Commonwealth Nation	Maseru	English
Liberia	Republic	Monrovia	English
Libya	Socialist People's Libyan Arab Jamahiriyah	Tripoli	Arabic, English
Liechtenstein	Principality	Vaduz	German
Luxembourg	Grand Duchy	Luxembourg	French, German
Madagascar	Democratic Republic	Antananarivo	French
Malawi	Republic, Commonwealth Nation	Lilongwe	English

Malaysia	Federation of States, Commonwealth Nation	Kuala Lumpur	English
Maldives	Republic	Malé	English
Mali	Republic	Bamako	French
Malta	Republic, Commonwealth Nation	Valletta	English, Maltese
Mauritania	Islamic Republic	Nouakchott	French, Arabic
Mauritius	Commonwealth Nation	Port Louis	English, French
Mexico	The United Mexican States, Federal Republic	Mexico City	Spanish
Monaco	Principality	Monaco	French
Mongolia	People's Republic	Ulaanbaatar	Russian
Morocco	Kingdom	Rabat	French, Spanish, Arabic
Mozambique	People's Republic	Maputo	Portuguese
Namibia	United Nations Trust Territory	Windhoek	Afrikaans, German, English
Nauru	Republic with special membership of the Commonwealth	Nauru	English
Nepal	Kingdom	Kathmandu	English
Netherlands, The	Kingdom	Amsterdam	Dutch
New Zealand	Commonwealth Nation	Wellington	English
Nicaragua	Republic	Managua	Spanish
Niger	Republic	Niamey	French
Nigeria	Federal Republic, Commonwealth Nation	Lagos	English
Norway	Kingdom	Oslo	Norwegian
Oman	Sultanate	Muscat	English, Arabic
Pakistan	Islamic Republic	Islamabad	English
Panama	Republic	Panamá City	Spanish, English
Papua New Guinea	Commonwealth Nation	Port Moresby	English

Paraguay	Republic	Asunción	Spanish
Peru	Republic	Lima	Spanish
Philippines	Republic	Manila	English, Spanish
Poland	People's Republic	Warszawa (Warsaw)	Polish
Portugal	Republic	Lisboa (Lisbon)	Portuguese
Puerto Rico	Self-governing commonwealth associated with the USA	San Juan	English, Spanish
Qatar	State	Doha	English, Arabic
Romania	Socialist Republic	Bucuresti (Bucharest)	Romanian
Rwanda	Republic	Kigali	French
St Kitts & Nevis	Independent. Commonwealth Nation	Basseterre	English
St Lucia	Commonwealth Nation	Castries	English, French
St Vincent	Commonwealth Nation	Kingston	English
San Marino	Republic	San Marino	Italian
São Tomé and Principe	Democratic Republic	São Tomé	Portuguese
Saudi Arabia	Kingdom	Riyadh	English, Arabic
Senegal	Republic	Dakar	French
Seychelles	Republic, Commonwealth Nation	Victoria	English, French
Sierra Leone	Republic, Commonwealth Nation	Freetown	English
Singapore	Republic, Commonwealth Nation	Singapore	English
Solomon Islands	Commonwealth Nation	Honiara	English
Somalia	The Somali Democratic Republic	Mogadiscio	English, Italian, Arabic
South Africa	Republic	Pretoria	English, Afrikaans
South Yemen	The People's Democratic Republic of Yemen	Aden	English, Arabic

Spain	The Spanish State, Kingdom	Madrid	Spanish
Sri Lanka	Democratic Socialist Republic, Commonwealth Nation	Colombo	English
Sudan	Democratic Republic	Khartoum	English, Arabic
Suriname	Republic	Paramaribo	Dutch, English
Swaziland	Kingdom, Commonwealth Nation	Mbabane	English
Sweden	Kingdom	Stockholm	Swedish
Switzerland	Republic, Confederation	Bern	German, French, Italian
Syria	Arab Republic	Damascus	English, Arabic
Taiwan	Republic of China	T'ai-pei (Taipei)	English, Mandarin
Tanzania	United Republic, Commonwealth Nation	Dodoma	English
Thailand	Kingdom	Krung Thep (Bangkok)	English
Togo	Republic	Lomé	French
Tonga	Kingdom, Commonwealth Nation	Nuku'alofa	English
Trinidad and Tobago	Republic, Commonwealth Nation	Port of Spain	English
Tunisia	Republic	Tunis	French, Arabic
Turkey	Republic	Ankara	Turkish
Tuvalu	Special membership of the Commonwealth	Funafuti	English
Uganda	Republic, Commonwealth Nation	Kampala	English
USSR	Union of Soviet Socialist Republics	Moskva (Moscow)	Russian
United Arab Emirates	Federal Union of seven Emirates	Abū Dhabi	English, Arabic
United Kingdom	United Kingdom of Great Britain and Northern Ireland	London	English
United States of America	Federal Republic	Washington DC	English

Uruguay	Republic	Montevideo	Spanish
Vanuatu	Republic, Commonwealth Nation	Vila	English, French
Vatican City	Ecclesiastical State	Vatican City	Italian
Venezuela	Republic	Caracas	Spanish
Vietnam	Socialist Republic	Hanoi	French
Western Samoa	Sovereign State, Commonwealth Nation	Apia	English
Yemen	Yemen Arab Republic	San´ā`	English, Arabic
Yugoslavia	Socialist Federal Republic	Beograd (Belgrade)	Serbo-Croat
Zaire	Republic	Kinshasa	French
Zambia	Republic, Commonwealth Nation	Lusaka	English
Zimbabwe	Republic, Commonwealth Nation	Harare	English

COMMERCIAL 'TERRITORIES' AND THEIR PARENT COUNTRIES

The list below shows territories (mainly islands) which are not listed as countries but which are of commercial significance.

The language for business purposes follows that of the parent country, as shown in the list on pp. 7–14.

Territory	*Parent country*
The Faeroes Greenland	Denmark
Corsica New Caledonia Réunion Tahiti and Moorea	France
Crete Rhodes	Greece
Sardinia Sicily	Italy
Netherland Antilles (Aruba, Curaçao, Bonaire)	The Netherlands
Azores Madeira	Portugal
Balearic Islands Canary Islands	Spain
Channel Islands Falkland Islands	United Kingdom
Alaska Hawaiian Islands	United States of America

BUSINESS LETTERS TO EUROPEAN COUNTRIES
Layout of this section

 *The envelope*

The correct address on the **envelope** for a:
   Mr
   Mrs
   Miss
   Doctor
   Engineer

written in the language of the recipient.

An example of a typical address including the name of a person, position in the organisation, the company name, the street, town and country in the correct order.

Names and addresses in each country are fictitious and given only as an example.

The language of the country

The correct opening salutation in the language of the country in a letter to a:
   Mr
   Mrs
   Miss
   Doctor
   Engineer
   Unnamed individual, and
      company
The correct closing phrase to an individual and a company/organisation.

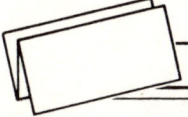

For letters written in English

The opening salutation in a letter to a:
   Mr
   Mrs
   Miss
   Doctor
   Engineer
   Unnamed individual, and
      company
The closing phrase to a named individual and company/organisation or unnamed individual.

Notes

Notes on the customs and practices of the country as they affect the writing of the envelope and the letter.

  Examples of titles and forms of address used when writing to State organisations in Eastern European countries.

AUSTRIA

THE ENVELOPE

Addressed to the equivalent of:

Mr	Initials	Surname	Herrn First Forename Surname
Mrs	"	"	Frau First Forename Surname
Miss	"	"	Frl. First Forename Surname
Doctor	"	"	Herrn *or* Frau Dr. First Forename Surname
Engineer	"	"	Herrn *or* Frau Dipl. Ing. First Forename Surname

Example of a typical address:

Company	Central-Wechselstuben AG
Position/	z.H. Herrn Kommerzialrat
Name	Dr. Erich Binder
Street	Himmelstr 27
Town	A – 1180 WIEN
Country	Austria

THE LETTER If written in German

Opening salutation corresponding to:

Dear Mr	Surname	Sehr geehrter Herr Surname!
Dear Mrs	"	Sehr geehrte Frau Surname!
Dear Miss	"	Sehr geehrtes Fräulein Surname!
Dear Doctor	"	Sehr geehrter Herr Dr. Surname!
Dear Engineer	"	Sehr geehrter Herr Dipl. Ing. Surname!
Dear Sir/Dear Madam		Sehr geehrter Herr! Sehr geehrte Frau!
Dear Sirs		Sehr geehrte Damen und Herren!

In the above examples the Doctor and Engineer are treated as male. Substitute geehrte Frau for females.

Closing phrase:

to an individual	Mit freundlichen Grüssen
to a company/organisation	" " "

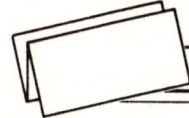

THE LETTER If written in English

Opening salutation to:

Mr	Dear Mr Surname, *or* Dear Herr Surname,	*Unusual to mix English and German when there are no other titles with Surname*
Mrs	Dear Mrs Surname, *or* Dear Frau Surname,	
Miss	Dear Miss Surname, *or* Dear Fräulein Surname,	
Doctor	Dear Dr Surname, *or* Dear Herr Dr. Surname, (or Frau)	
Engineer	Dear Mr, Mrs, Miss Surname *or* Dear Herr Dipl. Ing. Surname, (or Frau)	
Unnamed person	Dear Sir, Dear Madam,	
Company/organisation	Dear Sirs,	

Closing phrase:

to a named individual	Yours sincerely,
to a company/organisation or unnamed individual	Yours faithfully,

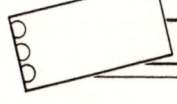

Notes on customs & practices

The envelope

The first forename is used only on the envelope in preference to initials. The omission of titles, positions or academic degrees is impolite on the envelope (and in the letter). The visiting card is usually a good indicator of how the recipient likes to be addressed.

Position is linked with the name. It is usual practice to write z.H. in front of the addressee (for the attention of) when his name is known.

The letter

On coming of age, unmarried women are addressed on the envelope and in the salutation as Frau and not Fräulein.

BELGIUM

THE ENVELOPE

Addressed to the equivalent of:

Mr	Initials	Surname	Monsieur First Forename Surname
Mrs	"	"	Madame First Forename Surname
Miss	"	"	Mademoiselle First Forename Surname
Doctor	"	"	Monsieur le Docteur First Forename Surname (*or* Madame, Mademoiselle)
Engineer	"	"	Monsieur First Forename Surname (*or* Madame, Mademoiselle)

Abbreviations M. (Monsieur), Mme. (Madame), Mlle. (Mademoiselle) are acceptable.

Example of a typical address:

Name	Monsieur J. Dupont
Position	Conseiller
Company	Sipla SA
Street	109 r de Molenboek
Town	1020 BRUXELLES
Country	Belgium

THE LETTER If written in French

Opening salutation corresponding to:

Dear Mr	Surname	Monsieur, *or if known*, Cher Monsieur,
Dear Mrs	"	Madame, *or if known*, Chère Madame,
Dear Miss	"	Mademoiselle,
Dear Doctor	"	Docteur,
Dear Engineer	"	Monsieur, *or if known*, Cher Monsieur,
Dear Sir, Dear Madam	"	Monsieur, Madame,
Dear Sirs	"	Messieurs,

In the above example the Engineer is treated as male. Substitute Madame or Mademoiselle if female.

(French speaking)

Closing phrase:

to an individual Je vous prie d'agréer, Monsieur, (*or title* in salutation) l'expression de mes sentiments distingués.

to company/organisation Je vous prie d'agréer, Messieurs, l'expression de mes/nos sentiments distingués.

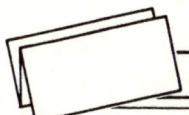

THE LETTER If written in English

Opening salutation to:

Mr	Dear Mr Surname, *or* Dear Monsieur Surname,
Mrs	Dear Mrs Surname, *or* Dear Madame Surname,
Miss	Dear Miss Surname, *or* Dear Mademoiselle Surname,
Doctor	Dear Dr Surname, *or* Dear Docteur,
Engineer	Dear Mr, Mrs, Miss Surname, *or* Dear Monsieur, Madame, Mademoiselle Surname,
Unnamed person	Dear Sir, Dear Madam,
Company/organisation	Dear Sirs,

Closing phrase:

to a named individual Yours sincerely,
to a company/organisation or unnamed individual Yours faithfully,

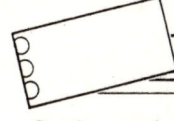

Notes on customs & practices

On the **envelope** initials or the first forename may be used. The first forename only is usually written, except where a forename is hyphenated, in which case it is written in full. The visiting card is usually a good indicator of how the recipient likes to be addressed. Except at senior level, it is the normal practice to write to the department of the firm or organisation and not to an individual. In the **letter** when writing in French the surname is always omitted in the salutation.

BELGIUM

THE ENVELOPE

Addressed to the equivalent of:

Mr	Initials	Surname	De Heer Initials Surname
Mrs	"	"	Mevrouw Initials Surname
Miss	"	"	Mejuffrouw Initials Surname
Doctor	"	"	Dokter Initials Surname
Engineer	"	"	Ingenieur Initials Surname

Example of a typical address:

Name	De Heer J. Janssen
Position	Adviseur
Company	Hendriks NV
Street	Turnhoutsebaan 354
Town	2018 ANTWERPEN
Country	Belgium

THE LETTER If written in Dutch

Opening salutation corresponding to:

Dear Mr	Surname	Geachte Heer Surname,
Dear Mrs	"	Geachte Mevrouw Surname,
Dear Miss	"	Geachte Mejuffrouw Surname,
Dear Doctor	"	Geachte Heer Surname,
Dear Engineer	"	Geachte Heer Surname,
Dear Sir, Dear Madam		Geachte Heer, Geachte Mevrouw,
Dear Sirs		Mijne Heren,

In the above examples both the Doctor and Engineer are treated as male. Substitute Mevrouw or Mejuffrouw for females.

Closing phrase:

| to an individual | Hoogachtend, or less formally, met vriendelÿke groeten hoogachtend, |
| to a company/organisation | Hoogachtend, |

(Flemish speaking)

THE LETTER If written in English

Opening salutation to:

Mr	Dear Mr Surname, *or*
	Dear Heer Surname,
Mrs	Dear Mrs Surname, *or*
	Dear Mevrouw Surname,
Miss	Dear Miss Surname, *or*
	Dear Mejuffrouw Surname,
Doctor	Dear Dr Surname, *or*
	Dear Heer Surname,
Engineer	Dear Mr, Mrs, Miss Surname, *or*
	Dear Heer Surname,
Unnamed person	Dear Sir, Dear Madam,
Company/organisation	Dear Sirs,

In the above examples both the Doctor and Engineer are treated as male. Substitute Mevrouw or Mejuffrouw for females.

Closing phrase:

to a named individual	Yours sincerely,
to a company/organisation or unnamed individual	Yours faithfully,

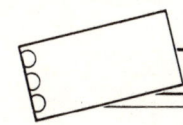

Notes on customs & practices

The envelope

Initials are used and not the forenames. Letters, eg, degrees, are used after the surname but only on the envelope. The visiting card is usually a good indicator of how the recipient likes to be addressed. Except at senior level, it is usual practice to write to the department of the firm or organisation and not to an individual.

The letter

Dokter, Ingenieur, etc., are not used in the salutation.

CYPRUS

THE ENVELOPE

Addressed to:

Mr	Initials	Surname
Mrs	"	"
Miss	"	"
Doctor	"	"

Example of a typical address:

Name	Mr K Paschalides
Position	
Company	Thrassyvoulou Lakis & Co Ltd
Street	17 Digenis Akritas Avenue
Town	NICOSIA
Country	Cyprus

THE LETTER If written in English

Opening salutation:

Dear Mr　　　　Surname,
Dear Mrs　　　　　"
Dear Miss　　　　"
Dear Doctor　　　"
Dear Sir
Dear Sirs

Closing phrase:

| to an individual | Yours sincerely, |
| to a company/organisation, | Yours faithfully, |

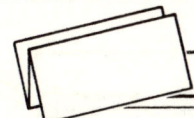

THE LETTER If written in English

Opening salutation to:

Mr
Mrs
Miss *See*
Doctor *above*
Unnamed person
Company/organisation

to a named individual Yours sincerely,
to a company/organisation or Yours faithfully,
unnamed individual

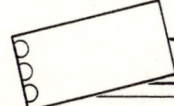

Notes on customs & practices

Most business letters from the UK are written in English and the practice is acceptable. The alternatives are to write in Greek or Turkish according to the native language of the recipient.

DENMARK

THE ENVELOPE

Addressed to the equivalent of:

Mr	Initials	Surname	Hr. Forename Surname
Mrs	"	"	Fru Forename Surname
			or Fr. Forename Surname
Miss	"	"	Frk Forename Surname
			or Fr. Forename Surname
Doctor	"	"	Hr Doktor Forename Surname (*for males*)
			Doktor Fr. Forename Surname (*for females*)
Engineer	"	"	Hr. Ingeniør Forename Surname

Example of a typical address:

Name	Hr. Direktør Bernhard Hansen
Position	(given in title above)
Company	Junkers Industries A/S
Street	Sankt Annæ Plads 5
Town	DK–1250 KØBENHAVN K
Country	Denmark

THE LETTER If written in Danish

Opening salutation corresponding to:

Dear Mr	Surname	Kære Hr. Surname,
Dear Mrs	"	Kære Fr. Surname,
Dear Miss	"	Kære Fr. Surname,
Dear Doctor	"	Kære Doktor Surname,
Dear Engineer	"	Kære Hr. Ingeniør Surname,
Dear Sir, Dear Madam, Dear Sirs		} *Not used*

Closing phrase:

to an individual
to a company/organisation
} *med venlig hilsen,*

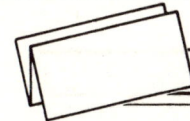

THE LETTER If written in English

Opening salutation to:

Mr	Dear Mr Surname, *or* Dear Hr. Surname,
Mrs	Dear Mrs Surname, *or* Dear Fr. Surname,
Miss	Dear Miss Surname, *or* Dear Fr. Surname,
Doctor	Dear Dr Surname, *or* Dear Doktor Surname,
Engineer	Dear Mr, Mrs, Miss Surname, *or* Dear Hr. Ingeniør Surname,
Unnamed person	Dear Sir, Dear Madam,
Company/organisation	Dear Sirs,

Closing phrase:

to a named individual	Yours sincerely,
to a company/organisation or unnamed individual	Yours faithfully,

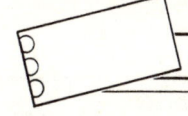

Notes on customs & practices

The envelope

The full forename(s) should always be written. The visiting card is usually a good indicator of how the individual likes to be addressed. It is usual practice, at least initially, to write to the department of the firm or organisation and not to an individual.

The letter

No salutation is used corresponding to the English Dear Sir, Dear Madam, Dear Sirs.

FINLAND

THE ENVELOPE

Addressed to the equivalent of:

(*see notes*)
Mr	Initials	Surname	Herra First Forename Surname (Herra *is abbreviated to* Hra)
Mrs	"	"	Rouva First Forename Surname
Miss	"	"	Neiti First Forename Surname
Doctor	"	"	Tohtori First Forename Surname (Tohtori *is abbreviated to* Tri)
Engineer	Diplomi-insinööri		First Forename Surname

Example of a typical address:

Name	Toimitusjohtaja Matti Metsä
Position	(*see notes*)
Company	Oy Soffco Ab
Street	Aallonkohina 8 D 77
Town	(SF-)02430 ESPOO
Country	Finland

Finnish and Swedish are the two official languages of Finland. Care is needed in selection in order to avoid offence to the recipient.

THE LETTER If written in Finnish

Opening salutation corresponding to:

Dear Mr	Surname
Dear Mrs	"
Dear Miss	"
Dear Doctor	"
Dear Engineer	"
Dear Sir	
Dear Sirs	

No salutation is used

Closing phrase:

to an individual	Parhain terveisin, *or* Ystävällisin terveisin,
to a company/organisation	Kunnioittavasti,

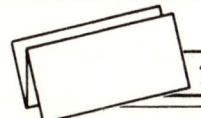

(Finnish speaking)

THE LETTER If written in English

Opening salutation to:

Mr	Dear Mr Surname, *or*
Mrs	Dear Mrs Surname, *or*
Miss	Dear Miss Surname, *or*
Doctor	Dear Dr Surname, *or*
Engineer	Dear Mr, Mrs, Miss Surname, *or*

} Dear Forename Surname,

Unnamed person	Dear Sir, Dear Madam,
Company/organisation	Dear Sirs,

} *or omit*

Closing phrase:

to a named individual — Yours sincerely,
to a company/organisation or — Yours faithfully,
unnamed individual

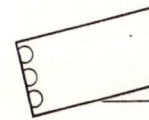

Notes on customs & practices

The envelope

The Finnish equivalent of Mr, Mrs etc, is used only if no other title is known. In the example above of a typical address, the word Toimitusjohtaja means Managing Director. Except at senior level, it is normal practice to write to the department of the firm or organisation and not to an individual.

The letter

In letters written in Finnish there are no salutations. In English, if an opening salutation is used, it is best to adopt normal British practice, although it is possible to omit the title, eg, Mr.

FINLAND

THE ENVELOPE

Addressed to the equivalent of:

Mr	Initials	Surname	Herr Forename Surname
Mrs	"	"	Fru Forename Surname
Miss	"	"	Fröken Forename Surname
Doctor	"	"	Doktor Forename Surname
Engineer	"	"	Diplomingenjör Forename Surname

Example of a typical address:

Name	*Depending upon visiting card*
	Diplomi—Insinööri Tapio Eskola
	or Diplomingenjör Tapio Eskola
Position	(*see notes*)
Company	Laborexin Oy
Street	Södrakajen 4 A
Town	(SF-)00130 HELSINKI
Country	Finland

As with the previous entry, Finnish and Swedish are the two official languages of Finland. Care is needed in selection in order to avoid offence to the recipient.

THE LETTER If written in Swedish

Opening salutation corresponding to:

Dear Mr	Surname	
Dear Mrs	"	
Dear Miss	"	
Dear Doctor	"	*No salutation is used*
Dear Engineer	"	
Dear Sir		
Dear Sirs		

Closing Phrase:

to an individual	Med vänliga hälsningar,
to a company/organisation	" " "

(Swedish speaking)

THE LETTER If written in English

Opening salutation to:

Mr	Dear Mr Surname, *or*
	Dear Herr Surname,
Mrs	Dear Mrs Surname, *or*
	Dear Fru Surname,
Miss	Dear Miss Surname, *or*
	Dear Fröken Surname,
Doctor	Dear Dr Surname,
Engineer	Dear Mr, Mrs, Miss Surname,
Unnamed person	Dear Sir, Dear Madam, } *or omit*
Company/organisation	Dear Sirs, }

Closing phrase:

to a named individual	Yours sincerely,
to a company/organisation or unnamed individual	Yours faithfully,

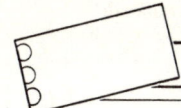

Notes on customs & practices

The envelope

When the recipient's visiting card shows a title, eg of position, it should be used. Except at senior level and where the recipient is known, it is normal practice to write to the department of the firm or organisation and not to an individual.

The letter

In letters written in Swedish there are no salutations.

FRANCE

THE ENVELOPE

Addressed to the equivalent of:

Mr	Initials	Surname	Monsieur First Forename Surname
Mrs	"	"	Madame First Forename Surname
Miss	"	"	Mademoiselle First Forename Surname
Doctor	"	"	Monsieur le Docteur First Forename Surname (*or* Madame, Mademoiselle)
Engineer	"	"	Monsieur First Forename Surname (*or* Madame, Mademoiselle)

Abbreviations M. (Monsieur), Mme. (Madame) and Mlle. (Mademoiselle) are acceptable.

Example of a typical address:

Name	Monsieur Paul Pierron
Position	Directeur Général
Company	Comiot SA
Street	29 rue de Missine
Town	F – 75017 PARIS
Country	France

THE LETTER If written in French

Opening salutation corresponding to:

Dear Mr	Surname	Monsieur, *or if known*, Cher Monsieur,
Dear Mrs	"	Madame, *or if known*, Chère Madame,
Dear Miss	"	Mademoiselle,
Dear Doctor	"	Docteur,
*Dear Engineer	"	Monsieur, *or if known*, Cher Monsieur,
Dear Sir, Dear Madam		Monsieur, Madame,
Dear Sirs		Messieurs,

Substitute Madame or Mademoiselle if female.

Closing phrase:

(to an individual)
Je vous prie d'agréer, Monsieur, (*or title in salutation*) l'expression de mes sentiments distingués.

(to a company/organisation)
Je vous prie d'agréer, Messieurs, l'expression de mes/nos sentiments distingués.

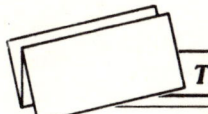

THE LETTER If written in English

Opening salutation to:

Mr	Dear Mr Surname, *or* Dear Monsieur Surname,
Mrs	Dear Mrs Surname, *or* Dear Madame Surname,
Miss	Dear Miss Surname, *or* Dear Mademoiselle Surname,
Doctor	Dear Dr Surname, *or* Dear Docteur,
Engineer	Dear Mr, Mrs, Miss Surname, *or* Dear Monsieur, Madame, Mademoiselle Surname,
Unnamed person	Dear Sir, Dear Madam,
Company/organisation	Dear Sirs,

Closing phrase:

to a named individual	Yours sincerely,
to a company/organisation or unnamed individual	Yours faithfully,

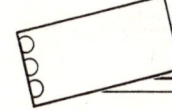

Notes on customs & practices

On the **envelope**, initials are used only when the forename is not known. The first forename only is used. A hyphenated forename is written in full. The visiting card is usually a good indicator of how the recipient likes to be addressed. Except at senior level, it is normal practice to write to the department of the firm or organisation and not to an individual. In the **letter**, when writing in French the surname is always omitted in the salutation.

WEST GERMANY

THE ENVELOPE

Addressed to the equivalent of:

Mr	Initials	Surname	Herrn Initials Surname
Mrs	"	"	Frau Initials Surname
Miss	"	"	Fräulein Initials Surname
Doctor	"	"	Herrn *or* Frau Dr. Initials Surname
Engineer	"	"	Herrn *or* Frau Dipl. Ing. Initials Surname

Example of a typical address:

Name	Herrn Generaldirektor Hans Becker
Position	(*see note*)
Company	Atika Cigarettenfabrik GmbH
Street	Parkstr.42
Town	D–2000 HAMBURG 62
Country	West Germany

THE LETTER If written in German

Opening salutation corrresponding to:

Dear Mr	Surname	Sehr geehrter Herr Surname,
Dear Mrs	"	Sehr geehrte Frau Surname,
Dear Miss	"	Sehr geehrtes Fräulein Surname,
*Dear Doctor	"	Sehr geehrter Herr Dr. Surname,
*Dear Engineer	"	Sehr geehrter Herr Dipl. Ing. Surname,
Dear Sir		(*see note*)
Dear Sirs		Sehr geehrte Damen und Herren,

Substitute Frau for females and alter geehrter to geehrte.

Closing phrase:

to an individual	Mit freundlichen Grüssen
to a company/organisation	Hochachtungsvoll

(Federal Republic of Germany)

THE LETTER If written in English

Opening salutation to:

Mr	Dear Mr Surname, *or* Dear Herr Surname,
Mrs	Dear Mrs Surname, *or* Dear Frau Surname,
Miss	Dear Miss Surname, *or* Dear Fräulein Surname,
Doctor	Dear Dr Surname, *or* Dear Herr Dr. Surname,
Engineer	Dear Mr, Mrs, Miss Surname, *or* Dear Herr Dipl. Ing. Surname,
Unnamed person	Dear Sir *or* Madam, *or* (see note)
Company/organisation	Dear Sirs,

In the above examples both the Doctor and Engineer are treated as male. Substitute Frau for females.

Closing phrase:

to a named individual	Yours sincerely,
to a company/organisation	Yours faithfully,

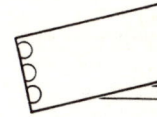

Notes on customs & practices

The envelope

The first forename may be used in substitution for the initial. The visiting card is usually a good indicator of how the recipient likes to be addressed. Position may be linked with the name. Except at senior level, it is normal practice to write to the department of the firm or organisation and not to an individual.

The letter

Whilst Dear Sir in English is acceptable, the German equivalent Sehr geehrter Herr is not polite. On coming of age, unmarried women are addressed on the envelope and in the salutation as Frau and not Fräulein.

GIBRALTAR

THE ENVELOPE

Addressed to:

Mr	Initials	Surname
Mrs	"	"
Miss	"	"
Doctor	"	"

Example of a typical address:

Name	Mr W D Tiley
Position	General Manager
Company	Dalsons Limited
Street	48 Main Street
Town	GIBRALTAR
Country	Gibraltar

THE LETTER If written in English

Opening salutation:

Dear Mr   Surname,
Dear Mrs   "
Dear Miss   "
Dear Doctor   "
Dear Sir
Dear Sirs

Closing phrase:

| to an individual | Yours sincerely, |
| to a company/organisation | Yours faithfully, |

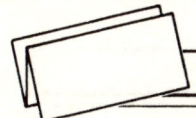

THE LETTER If written in English

Opening salutation:

Mr
Mrs
Miss   *See*
Doctor   *above*
Unnamed person
Company/organisation

Closing phrase:

to a named individual   Yours sincerely,
to a company/organisation or   Yours faithfully,
unnamed individual

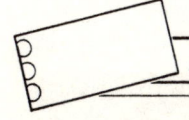

Notes on customs & practices

Most business letters from the UK are written in English and this is acceptable practice. The alternative is to write in Spanish since most recipients are bilingual.

GREECE

THE ENVELOPE

Addressed to the equivalent of:

Mr	Initials	Surname	Κύριο Initials Surname *or* Κον Initials Surname (*Abbreviation*)
Mrs	"	"	Κυρία Initials Surname (*or Abbreviated*) Κα Initials Surname
Miss	"	"	Δίδα Initials Surname
Doctor	"	"	Κον Initials Surname Ιατρό
Engineer	"	"	Κον Initials Surname Μηχανικό

Example of a typical address:

Name	Mr P Skendros		Κον Π. Σκένδρον,
Company	Institut National d'Assurances de Grece SA	*or*,	Ινστιτούτον Εθνικής Ασφάλειας Ελλάδος Σ.Α.,
Street	6 Ag Constantinou		Οδός Αγίου Κωνσταντίνου αρ. 6,
Town	ATHINAI		Αθήνα.
Country	Greece		Greece

THE LETTER If written in Greek

Opening salutation corresponding to:

Dear Mr	Surname	Αξιότιμε Κύριε Surname,
Dear Mrs	"	Αξιότιμη Κυρία Surname,
Dear Miss	"	Αξιότιμη Δίδα Surname,
Dear Doctor	"	Αξιότιμε Κύριε Surname,
Dear Engineer	"	Αξιότιμε Κύριε Surname,
Dear Sir		Αξιότιμε Κύριε
Dear Sirs		Αξιότιμοι Κύριοι,

Closing phrase:

to an individual	Μ'εκτίμηση
to a company/organisation	Με τιμή

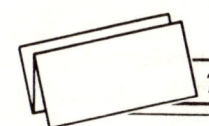

THE LETTER If written in English

Opening salutation to:

Mr	Dear Mr Surname, *or*
	Dear Κύριο Surname,
Mrs	Dear Mrs Surname *or*
	Dear Κυρία Surname,
Miss	Dear Miss Surname, *or*
	Dear Δίδα Surname,
Doctor	Dear Dr Surname,
Engineer	Dear Mr, Mrs, Miss Surname,
Unnamed person	Dear Sir, Dear Madam,
Company/organisation	Dear Sirs,

Closing phrase:

to a named individual	Yours sincerely,
to a company/organisation or unnamed individual	Yours faithfully,

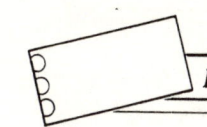

Notes on customs & practices

The envelope

Initials or forenames may be used. The visiting card is usually a good indicator of how the recipient likes to be addressed. Except at senior level, it is normal practice to write to the department of the firm or organisation and not to an individual.

The envelope in the above example shows the name and address in both Roman and Greek type.

ICELAND

THE ENVELOPE

Addressed to the equivalent of:

Mr	Initials	Surname	Herra Forename Surname *or* Hr. Forename Surname
Mrs	"	"	Fru Forename Surname
Miss	"	"	Frøken Forename Surname *or* Frk. Forename Surname
Doctor	"	"	} *Use title only if shown*
Engineer	"	"	} *on visiting card*

Example of a typical address:

Name	Fru Inga Bjornsson
Position	Framkvæmdarstjóri
Company	Jöfunn H/F
Street	Klapparstigur 28
Town	101 REYKJAVIK
Country	Iceland

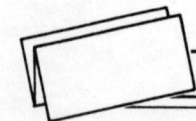

THE LETTER If written in Icelandic

Opening salutation corresponding to:

Dear Mr	Surname	Kæri Herra Surname,
Dear Mrs	"	Kæra Fru Surname,
Dear Miss	"	Kæra Frøken Surname,
Dear Doctor	"	Kæri *or* Kæra Dr. Surname,
Dear Engineer	"	Kæri *or* Kæra Herra, Fru or Frøken Surname,
Dear Sir		} Usually omitted
Dear Sirs		

Closing phrase:

to an individual } Virðingarfyllst
to a company/organisation

THE LETTER If written in English

Opening salutation to:

Mr	Dear Mr Surname, *or* Dear Herra Surname,
Mrs	Dear Mrs Surname, *or* Dear Fru Surname,
Miss	Dear Miss Surname, *or* Dear Frøken Surname,
Doctor	Dear Dr Surname, *or* Dear Dr. Surname,
Engineer	Dear Mr, Mrs, Miss Surname, *or* Dear Herra, Fru, Frøken Surname,
Unnamed person	Dear Sir, Dear Madam,
Company/organisation	Dear Sirs,

Closing phrase:

to a named individual	Yours sincerely,
to a company/organisation or unnamed individual	Yours faithfully,

Notes on customs & practices

The envelope

If the forename is not known, use initials. The visiting card is usually a good indicator of how the recipient likes to be addressed and his title and letters/abbreviations should be followed on the envelope. It is usual practice, at least initially, to write to the department of the firm or organisation and not to an individual.

The letter

The opening salutation to an individual may be omitted. There is no equivalent to the English Dear Sir or Dear Sirs.

ITALY

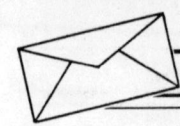

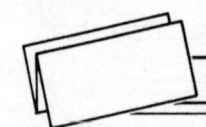

THE ENVELOPE

Addressed to the equivalent of:

Mr	Initials	Surname	Egregio Signor Initials Surname *or* Egr. Sig. Initials Surname
Mrs	"	"	Gentile Signora Initials Surname *or* Gent.ma Sig.ra Initials Surname
Miss	"	"	Gentile Signorina Initials Surname *or* Gent.ma Sig.na Initials Surname
Doctor	"	"	Egregio Dottor Initials Surname *or* Egr. Dott. Initials Surname
Engineer	"	"	Egregio Ingegner Initials Surname *or* Egr. Ing. Initials Surname

The above assumes the Doctor and Engineer are both male. Write Gentile Dottoressa Initials Surname and Gentile Ingegner initials Surname if female.

Example of a typical address:

Name	Egr.Sig. G. Valgimigli
Position	Direttore Servizio Vendite
Company	Fratelli Borella S.p.A.
Street	Via Testi, 36
Town	20126 MILANO
Country	Italy

THE LETTER If written in Italian

Opening salutation corresponding to:

Dear Mr	Surname	Egregio Signor Surname,
Dear Mrs	"	Gentile Signora Surname,
Dear Miss	"	Gentile Signorina Surname,
Dear Doctor	"	Egregio Dottor Surname,
Dear Engineer	"	Egregio Ingegner Surname,
Dear Sir		Egregio Signore,
Dear Sirs		Egregio Signori,

The above assumes the Doctor and Engineer are both male. Write Gentile Dottoressa Surname and Gentile Ingegner Surname if female.

Closing phrase:

to an individual   Distinti saluti, *or* La prego di
                                  gradire i miei piu cordiali saluti
to a company/organisation   Distinti saluti

THE LETTER If written in English

Opening salutation to:

Mr	Dear Mr Surname, *or*
	Dear Signor Surname,
Mrs	Dear Mrs Surname, *or*
	Dear Signora Surname,
Miss	Dear Miss Surname, *or*
	Dear Signorina Surname,
Doctor	Dear Dr Surname, *or*
	Dear Dottor Surname,
Engineer	Dear Mr, Mrs, Miss Surname, *or*
	Dear Ingegner Surname,
Un-named person	Dear Sir or Madam,
Company/organisation	Dear Sirs,

The above assumes the Doctor is male. Write Dear Dottoressa Surname if female.

Closing phrase:

to a named individual   Yours sincerely,
to a company/organisation or   Yours faithfully,
unnamed individual

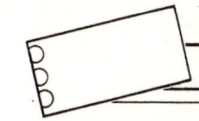

Notes on customs & practices

The envelope

It is the custom to abbreviate the titles but only on the envelope. The first forename may be used in place of an initial. The visiting card is usually a good indicator of how the recipient likes to be addressed. Except at senior level, it is normal practice to write to the department of the firm or organisation and not to an individual.

The letter

In the salutation Egregio Signore is sometimes omitted and Egregio Signori is often omitted.

LIECHTENSTEIN

THE ENVELOPE

Addressed to the equivalent of:

Mr	Initials	Surname	Herrn
			Initials Surname
Mrs	"	"	Frau
			Initials Surname
Miss	"	"	Fräulein
			Initials Surname
Doctor	"	"	Herrn *or* Frau
			Dr. Initials Surname
Engineer	"	"	Herrn *or* Frau
			Dipl. Ing. Initials Surname

Example of a typical address:

Name	Herrn
	Josef Marogg
Position	*(see note)*
Company	Loppacher Seger AG
Street	Mareestrasse 14
Town	VADUZ
Country	Liechtenstein

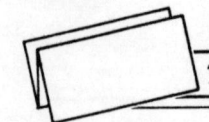

THE LETTER If written in German

Opening salutation corresponding to:

Dear Mr	Surname	Sehr geehrter Herr Surname,
Dear Mrs	"	Sehr geehrte Frau Surname,
Dear Miss	"	Sehr geehrtes Fräulein Surname,
Dear Doctor	"	Sehr geehrter Herr Dr. Surname,
Dear Engineer	"	Sehr geehrter Herr Dipl. Ing. Surname,
Dear Sir		*(see note)*
Dear Sirs		Sehr geehrte Damen und Herren,

In the above examples both the Doctor and Engineer are treated as male. Substitute Frau for females and alter geehrter to geehrte.

Closing phrase:

to an individual Mit freundlichen Grüssen
to a company/organisation Hochachtungsvoll

THE LETTER If written in English

Opening salutation to:

Mr	Dear Mr Surname, *or*
	Dear Herr Surname,
Mrs	Dear Mrs Surname, *or*
	Dear Frau Surname,
Miss	Dear Miss Surname, *or*
	Dear Fräulein Surname,
*Doctor	Dear Dr Surname, *or*
	Dear Herr Dr. Surname,
*Engineer	Dear Mr, Mrs, Miss Surname, *or*
	Dear Herr Dipl.Ing. Surname,
Unnamed person	Dear Sir, *or* Madam, *or*
	(*see note*)
Company/organisation	Dear Sirs,

Substitute Frau for females.

Closing phrase:

to a named individual Yours sincerely,
to a company/organisation Yours faithfully,

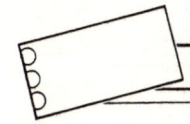

Notes on customs & practices

On the **envelope**, the first forename may be used in substitution for the initial. The visiting card is usually a good indicator of how the recipient likes to be addressed. Position may be linked with the name. Except at senior level, it is normal practice to write to the department of the firm or organisation and not to an individual. In the **letter**, whilst Dear Sir in English is acceptable, the German equivalent, Sehr geehrter Herr is not polite. On coming of age, unmarried women are addressed on the envelope and in the salutation as Frau and not Fräulein.

LUXEMBOURG

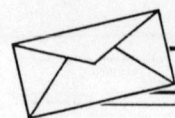

THE ENVELOPE

Addressed to the equivalent of:

Mr	Initials	Surname	Monsieur First Forename Surname
Mrs	"	"	Madame First Forename Surname
Miss	"	"	Mademoiselle First Forename Surname
Doctor	"	"	Monsieur le Docteur First Forename Surname (*or* Madame, Mademoiselle)
Engineer	"	"	Monsieur First Forename Surname (*or* Madame, Mademoiselle)

Abbreviations M. (Monsieur), Mme. (Madame), Mlle. (Mademoiselle) are acceptable.

Example of a typical address:

Name	Monsieur Michel Nage
Position	Directeur Général
Company	Multaler et Cie
Street	42 rue Royale
Town	2954 LUXEMBOURG
Country	Luxembourg

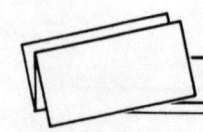

THE LETTER If written in French

Opening salutation corresponding to:

Dear Mr	Surname	Monsieur, *or* if known, Cher Monsieur,
Dear Mrs	"	Madame, *or* if known, Chère Madame,
Dear Miss	"	Mademoiselle,
Dear Doctor	"	Docteur,
*Dear Engineer	"	Monsieur, *or* if known, Cher Monsieur,
Dear Sir, Dear Madam		Monsieur, Madame,
Dear Sirs		Messieurs,

*Substitute Madame or Mademoiselle if female.

(French speaking)

Closing phrase:

to an individual
Je vous prie d'agréer, Monsieur, (or title in salutation) l'expression de mes sentiments distingués.

to company/organisation
Je vous prie d'agréer, Messieurs, l'expression de mes/nos sentiments distingués.

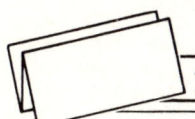

THE LETTER If written in English

Opening salutation to:

Mr
Dear Mr Surname, *or*
Dear Monsieur Surname,

Mrs
Dear Mrs Surname, *or*
Dear Madame Surname,

Miss
Dear Miss Surname, *or*
Dear Mademoiselle Surname,

Doctor
Dear Dr Surname, *or*
Dear Docteur,

Engineer
Dear Mr, Mrs, Miss Surname, *or*
Dear Monsieur, Madame, Mademoiselle Surname,

Unnamed person
Dear Sir, Dear Madam,

Company/organisation
Dear Sirs,

Closing phrase:

to a named individual
Yours sincerely,

to a company/organisation or unnamed individual
Yours faithfully,

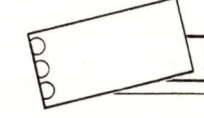

Notes on customs & practices

On the **envelope**, initials are used only when the forename is not known. The first forename only is usually written except where a forename is hyphenated. Except at senior level, it is the normal practice to write to the department of an organisation and not an individual.

LUXEMBOURG

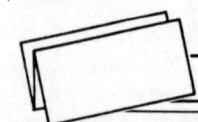

THE ENVELOPE

Addressed to the equivalent of:

Mr	Initials	Surname	Herrn Initials Surname
Mrs	"	"	Frau Initials Surname
Miss	"	"	Fräulein Initials Surname
Doctor	"	"	Herrn *or* Frau
			Dr. Initials Surname
Engineer	"	"	Herrn *or* Frau
			Dipl. Ing. Initials Surname

Example of a typical address:

Name	Herrn Direktor
	Hans Nagle
Position	*(see note)*
Company	Muller Wegener S.A.R.L.
Street	21 rue De Hollerich
Town	2950 LUXEMBOURG
Country	Luxembourg

THE LETTER If written in German

Opening salutation corresponding to:

Dear Mr	Surname	Sehr geehrter Herr Surname!
Dear Mrs	"	Sehr geehrte Frau Surname!
Dear Miss	"	Sehr geehrtes Fräulein Surname!
*Dear Doctor	"	Sehr geehrter Herr Dr. Surname!
*Dear Engineer	"	Sehr geehrter Herr Dipl. Ing. Surname!
Dear Sir		*(see note)*
Dear Sirs		Sehr geehrte Damen und Herren!

Substitute Frau for females and alter geehrter to geehrte.

(German speaking)

Closing phrase:

to an individual Mit freundlichen Grüssen
to a company/organisation Hochachtungsvoll

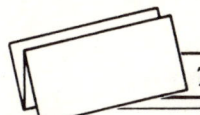

THE LETTER If written in English

Opening salutation to:

Mr	Dear Mr Surname, *or* Dear Herr Surname,
Mrs	Dear Mrs Surname, *or* Dear Frau Surname,
Miss	Dear Miss Surname, *or* Dear Fräulein Surname,
*Doctor	Dear Dr Surname, *or* Dear Herr Dr. Surname,
*Engineer	Dear Mr, Mrs, Miss Surname *or* Dear Herr Dipl. Ing. Surname,
Unnamed person	Dear Sir *or* Madam, *or* (see note)
Company/organisation	Dear Sirs,

Substitute Frau for female.

Closing phrase:

to a named individual Yours sincerely,
to a company/organisation Yours faithfully,

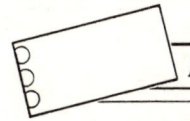

Notes on customs & practices

On the **envelope**, the first forename may be used in substitution for the initial. The visiting card is usually a good indicator of how the recipient likes to be addressed. Position may be linked with the name. Except at senior level, it is normal practice to write to the department of the firm or organisation and not to an individual. In the **letter**, whilst 'Dear Sir' in English is acceptable, the German equivalent 'Sehr geehrter Herr' is not polite. On coming of age, unmarried women are addressed on the envelope and in the salutation as Frau and not Fräulein.

MALTA G.C.

THE ENVELOPE

Addressed to the equivalent of:

Mr	Initials	Surname	Sur Forename Surname
Mrs	"	"	Sinjura Forename Surname
Miss	"	"	Sinjurina Forename Surname
Doctor	"	"	Dr Forename Surname
Engineer	"	"	Sur
			Sinjura Forename Surname
			Sinjurina

Example of a typical address:

Name	Sur Raymond Gera
Position	
Company	Charles Darmanin & Co Ltd
Street	36 St Paul's Street
Town	VALLETTA
Country	Malta

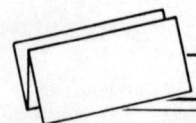

THE LETTER If written in Maltese

Opening salutation corresponding to:

Dear Mr	Surname	Ghaziz Sur Surname,
Dear Mrs	"	Ghaziz Sinjura Surname,
Dear Miss	"	Ghaziz Sinjurina Surname,
Dear Doctor	"	Ghaziz Dr. Surname,
Dear Engineer	"	Ghaziz Sur, Sinjura, Sinjurina Surname,
Dear Sir, Dear Madam,		Ghaziz Sinjur, Ghaziz Sinjura,
Dear Sirs		Ghaziz Sinjuri

Closing phrase:

to an individual
to a company/organisation } Dejjem tieghek,

THE LETTER If written in English

Opening salutation to:

Mr	Dear Mr Surname,
Mrs	Dear Mrs Surname,
Miss	Dear Miss Surname,
Doctor	Dear Dr Surname,
Engineer	Dear Mr, Mrs, Miss Surname,
Unnamed person	Dear Sir,
Company/organisation	Dear Sirs,

Closing phrase:

to a named individual	Yours sincerely,
to a company/organisation or unnamed individual	Yours faithfully,

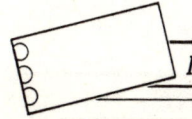

Notes on customs & practices

Business letters from the UK are usually written in English. The envelope, in the above example, would be addressed to Mr Raymond Gera. The opening salutation and the closing phrase would be in English and it would be incorrect to begin, for example 'Dear Sur Gera'.

NETHERLANDS

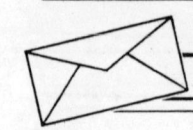

THE ENVELOPE

Addressed to the equivalent of:

Mr	Initials	Surname	De Heer Initials Surname
Mrs	"	"	Mevrouw Initials Surname
Miss	"	"	Mejuffrouw Initials Surname
Doctor	"	"	Dokter Initials Surname
Engineer	"	"	Ingenieur Initials Surname

Example of a typical address:

Name	De Heer A Rinckes
Position	Directeur
Company	Bekaert Netherland NV
Street	Kastanyelaan 53
Town	DEN HAAG
Country	Netherlands

THE LETTER If written in Dutch

Opening salutation corresponding to:

Dear Mr	Surname	Geachte Heer Surname,
Dear Mrs	"	Geachte Mevrouw Surname,
Dear Miss	"	Geachte Mejuffrouw Surname,
Dear Doctor	"	Geachte Heer Surname,
Dear Engineer	"	Geachte Heer Surname,
Dear Sir, Dear Madam		Geachte Heer, Geachte Mevrouw,
Dear Sirs		Mijne Heren,

In the above examples both the Doctor and Engineer are treated as male. Substitute Mevrouw or Mejuffrouw for females.

Closing phrase:

to an individual	Hoogachtend, *or less formally*, met vriendelÿke groeten hoogachtend,
to a company/organisation	Hoogachtend,

THE LETTER If written in English

Opening salutation to:

Mr	Dear Mr Surname, *or* Dear Heer Surname,
Mrs	Dear Mrs Surname, *or* Dear Mevrouw Surname,
Miss	Dear Miss Surname, *or* Dear Mejuffrouw Surname,
Doctor	Dear Dr Surname, *or* Dear Heer Surname,
Engineer	Dear Mr, Mrs, Miss Surname, *or* Dear Heer Surname,
Unnamed person	Dear Sir, Dear Madam,
Company/organisation	Dear Sirs,

In the above examples both the Dr and Engineer are treated as male. Substitute Mevrouw or Mejuffrouw for females.

Closing phrase:

to a named individual	Yours sincerely,
to a company/organisation or unnamed individual	Yours faithfully,

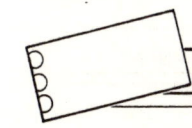

Notes on customs & practices

The envelope

Initials are used and not the forenames. Letters, eg degrees, are used after the surname but only on the envelope. The visiting card is usually a good indicator of how the recipient likes to be addressed. Except at senior level, it is usual practice to write to the department of the firm or organisation and not to an individual.

The letter

Dokter, Ingenieur, etc, are not used in the salutation. The opening salutation which is partly in English and partly in Dutch as given above is very unusual in the Netherlands and it is probably preferable to write entirely in English or entirely in Dutch.

NORWAY

THE ENVELOPE

Addressed to the equivalent of:

(see notes)

Mr	Initials	Surname	Herr Forename Surname *or* Hr. Forename Surname
Mrs	"	"	Fru Forename Surname *or* Fr. Forename Surname
Miss	"	"	Frøken Forename Surname *or* Fr. Forename Surname
Doctor	"	"	} Use title only if shown on visiting card
Engineer	"	"	

Example of a typical address:

Name	Hr. Odd Johannessen
Position	Adm. direktør
Company	Tavel Invest A/S
Street	Torgalmenning 2
Town	N–5002 BERGEN
Country	Norway

THE LETTER If written in Norwegian

Opening salutation corresponding to:

Dear Mr	Surname	Kjære Herr Surname,
Dear Mrs	"	Kjære Fru Surname, } usually omitted
Dear Miss	"	Kjære Frøken Surname,

Dear Doctor "
Dear Engineer "   } omit
Dear Sir
Dear Sirs

Closing phrase:

to an individual	Med Vennlig hilsen,
to a company/organisation	Med Hilsen,

THE LETTER If written in English

Opening salutation to:

Mr	Dear Mr Surname, *or* Dear Hr. Surname,
Mrs	Dear Mrs Surname, *or* Dear Fru Surname,
Miss	Dear Miss Surname, *or* Dear Frøken Surname,
Doctor	Dear Dr Surname, *or* Dear Dr. Surname,
Engineer	Dear Mr, Mrs, Miss Surname, *or* Dear Hr, Fru, Frøken Surname,
Unnamed person	Dear Sir, Dear Madam,
Company/organisation	Dear Sirs,

Closing phrase:

to a named individual	Yours sincerely,
to a company/organisation or unnamed individual	Yours faithfully,

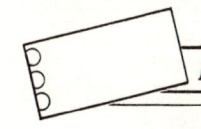

Notes on customs & practices

The envelope

When addressed to an individual it is normal practice within the country to omit titles and write the forename(s) and surname only. If forenames are not known, use initials. The visiting card is usually a good indicator of how the recipient likes to be addressed and his title and letters/abbreviations should be followed on the envelope. It is normal practice at least initially, to write to the department of the firm or organisation and not to an individual.

The letter

Opening salutations are usually omitted. Otherwise use Kjære (meaning Dear) followed by, for example, Herr or Hr.

PORTUGAL

THE ENVELOPE

Addressed to the equivalent of:

Mr	Initials	Surname	Exm^o Senhor Forenames Surname
Mrs	"	"	Exm^a Senhora D. Forenames Surname(s)
Miss	"	"	(*Not used in business letters*)
Doctor	"	"	Exm^o Senhor Dr. *or* Exm^a Senhora Dr^a Forenames Surname
Engineer	"	"	Exm^o Senhor Eng. *or* Exm^a Senhora Eng.^{a} Forenames Surname

Example of a typical address:

Name	Exm^o Senhor Eng. Teixeira Lopo
Position	Director
Company	Almor Viegas Lda
Street	Av da Liberdade 126
Town	1398 LISBOA
Country	Portugal

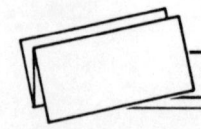

THE LETTER If written in Portuguese

Opening salutation corresponding to:

Dear Mr	Surname	Exm^o Senhor Forenames Surname
Dear Mrs	"	Exm^a Senhora D. Forenames Surname(s)
Dear Miss	"	(Not used in business letters)
Dear Doctor	"	Exm^o Senhor Dr. *or* Exm^a Senhora Dr.ª Forenames Surname(s)
Dear Engineer	"	Exm^o Senhor Eng. *or* Exm^a Senhora Eng.^{a} Forenames Surname(s)
Dear Sir, Dear Madam,		Exm^o Senhor *or* Exm^a Senhora
Dear Sirs		Exm^{o}s Senhores

Closing phrase:

(to an individual)
Com os melhores cumprimentos,
subscrevemo–me,
De V. Ex^a
Atentamente

(to a company/organisation)
Com os melhores cumprimentos,
subscrevemo–nos,
De V. Ex^a
Atentamente

THE LETTER If written in English

Opening salutation to:

Mr	Dear Mr Forenames Surname, *or* Dear Senhor Forenames Surname
Mrs	Dear Mrs Forenames Surname(s), *or* Dear Senhora D. Forenames Surname(s)
Miss	(*not used in business*)
Doctor	Dear Dr Forenames Surname(s), *or* Dear Senhor Dr. *or* Senhora Dr.ª Forenames Surname(s)
Engineer	Dear Mr/Mrs Forenames Surname(s), *or* Dear Senhor Eng. *or* Senhora Eng.^{a} Forenames Surname(s)
Unnamed person	Dear Sir, *or* Madam,
Company/organisation	Dear Sirs,

Closing phrase:

to a named individual	Yours sincerely,
to a company/organisation or unnamed individual	Yours faithfully,

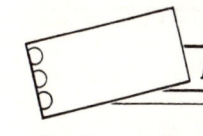

Notes on customs & practices

On the **envelope**, unless there are more than four, always use forenames rather than initials (also in the salutation). A wife can choose whether to take her husband's surname or not. If so, it is added to her existing family name. The male has just his family name. The visiting card is usually a good indicator of how the recipient likes to be addressed. Except at senior level, it is normal practice to write to the department of the firm or organisation and not to an individual. In the **letter**, if writing to a person one knows it is the custom to substitute Caro for Exm^o Senhor/Exm^a Senhora etc followed by the forenames and surname. In business address a Miss as a Mrs.

SPAIN

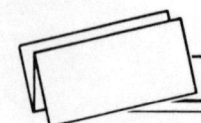

THE ENVELOPE

Addressed to the equivalent of:

Mr	Initials	Surname	Sr.D.Initials Surnames
			(Sr. *is abbreviation of* Señor)
Mrs	"	"	Sra.Doña Initials Surnames
			(Sra. *is abbreviation of* Señora)
Miss	"	"	Srta. Initials Surnames
			(Srta. *is abbreviation of* Señorita)
Doctor	"	"	Sr.D. Initials Surnames
			(*if male, otherwise use* Sra.Doña *or* Srta.)
Engineer	"	"	Sr.D. Initials Surnames
			(*if male, otherwise use* Sra.Doña *or* Srta.)

Example of a typical address:

Name	Sr.D.Agustín Laborda Villiers
Position	(*unusual on envelope*)
Company	Aceros Atlas, SA
Street	Av Meridiana, 273
Town	BARCELONA – 11
Country	Spain

THE LETTER If written in Spanish

Opening salutation corresponding to:

Dear Mr	Surname	Muy Sr.mío:
Dear Mrs	"	Muy Sra:mía:
Dear Miss	"	Srta.First Surname:
Dear Doctor	"	Muy Sr.mío: *or*
		Sr.Doctor First
		Surname:
Dear Engineer	"	Muy Sr.mío: *or*
		Sr.Ingeniero First
		Surname:
Dear Sir or Madam		Muy Sr.mío: *or* Muy Sra.mía:
Dear Sirs		Muy Srs.míos:

In the above examples both the Dr and Engineer are treated as male. Substitute Sra. or Srta. for females.

Closing phrase:

to an individual	Le saluda atentamente:
to a company/organisation	Le saluda atentamente:

THE LETTER If written in English

Opening salutation to:

Mr	Dear Mr First Surname, *or* Dear Sr. First Surname,
Mrs	Dear Mrs First Surname, *or* Dear Sra. First Surname,
Miss	Dear Miss First Surname, *or* Dear Srta. First Surname,
Doctor	Dear Dr First Surname, *or* Dear Sr.Doctor First Surname,
Engineer	Dear Mr, Mrs, Miss First Surname, *or* Dear Sr.Ingeniero First Surname,
Unnamed person	Dear Sir or Madam,
Company/organisation	Dear Sirs,

In the above examples both the Dr and Engineer are treated as males. Substitute Sra. or Srta. for females.

Closing phrase:

to a named individual	Yours sincerely,
to a company/organisation or unnamed individual	Yours faithfully,

Notes on customs & practices

On the **envelope**, the full title or abbreviations may be used. Spaniards have two surnames both of which should be used. The visiting card is usually a good indicator of how the recipient likes to be addressed. Except at senior level, it is normal practice to write to the department of the firm or organisation and not to an individual. In the **letter**, in the salutations where a surname is used, it is the first surname only which is written. The salutations given are those employed when the recipient is little known. When well known use 'Estimado Pablo:' or 'Apreciado amigo:' and to close informally 'Un saludo de tu amigo:'

SWEDEN

THE ENVELOPE

Addressed to the equivalent of:

Mr	Initials	Surname	Herr Forename Surname
Mrs	"	"	Fru Forename Surname
Miss	"	"	Fröken Forename Surname
Doctor	"	"	Doktor Forename Surname
Engineer	"	"	Ingenjör Forename Surname

Example of a typical address:

Name	Herr Direktör Stephan Evensson
Position	
Company	Svenskä Handelsbank
Street	Nybrokajen 9
Town	S – 111 39 STOCKHOLM
Country	Sweden

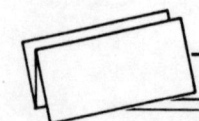

THE LETTER If written in Swedish

Opening salutation corresponding to:

Dear Mr   Surname
Dear Mrs   "
Dear Miss   "
Dear Doctor   "   *No salutation is used*
Dear Engineer   "
Dear Sir / Madam
Dear Sirs

Closing phrase:

to an individual   Med vänliga hälsningar,
to a company/organisation   "   "   "

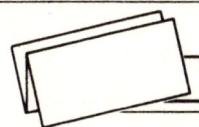

THE LETTER If written in English

Opening salutation to:

Mr	Dear Mr Surname, *or*
	Dear Herr Surname,
Mrs	Dear Mrs Surname, *or*
	Dear Fru Surname,
Miss	Dear Miss Surname, *or*
	Dear Fröken Surname,
Doctor	Dear Dr Surname,
Engineer	Dear Mr, Mrs, Miss Surname,
Unnamed person	Dear Sir, Dear Madam, } *or omit*
Company/organisation	Dear Sirs,

Closing phrase:

to a named individual	Yours sincerely,
to a company/organisation or unnamed individual	Yours faithfully,

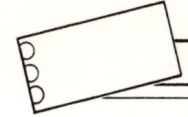

Notes on customs & practices

The envelope

When the recipient's visiting card shows a title eg of position, it should be used. Except at senior level and where the recipient is known, it is normal practice to write to the department of the firm or organisation and not to an individual.

The letter

In letters written in Swedish there are no salutations.

SWITZERLAND

THE ENVELOPE

Addressed to the equivalent of:

Mr	Initials	Surname	Monsieur First Forename Surname
			(M. *is the abbreviation of* Monsieur)
Mrs	"	"	Madame First Forename Surname
			(Mme. *is the abbreviation of* Madame)
Miss	"	"	Mademoiselle First Forename Surname
			(Mlle. *is the abbreviation of* Mademoiselle)
Doctor	"	"	Monsieur le Docteur First Forename Surname
			(*or* Madame, Mademoiselle)
Engineer	"	"	Monsieur First Forename Surname
			(*or* Madame, Mademoiselle)

Example of a typical address:

Name	Monsieur
	Jean Bouguin
Position	Directeur
Company	Sauter SA
Street	2 rue des Beaux-Arts
Town	2005 NEUCHATEL
Country	Switzerland

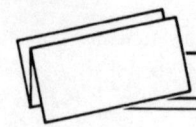

THE LETTER If written in French

Opening salutation corresponding to:

Dear Mr	Surname	Monsieur, *or* if known, Cher Monsieur,
Dear Mrs	"	Madame, *or* if known, Chère Madame,
Dear Miss	"	Mademoiselle,
Dear Doctor	"	Docteur,
*Dear Engineer	"	Monsieur, *or* if known, Cher Monsieur,
Dear Sir, Dear Madam		Monsieur, Madame,
Dear Sirs		Messieurs,

*Substitute Madame or Mademoiselle if female.

(French speaking)

Closing phrase:

to an individual	Je vous prie d'agréer, Monsieur, (*or title in salutation*) l'expression de mes sentiments distingués.
to a company/organisation	Je vous prie d'agréer, Messieurs, l'expression de mes/nos sentiments distingués.

THE LETTER If written in English

Opening salutation to:

Mr	Dear Mr Surname, *or* Dear Monsieur Surname,
Mrs	Dear Mrs Surname, *or* Dear Madame Surname,
Miss	Dear Miss Surname, *or* Dear Mademoiselle Surname,
Doctor	Dear Dr Surname, *or* Dear Docteur,
Engineer	Dear Mr, Mrs, Miss Surname, *or* Dear Monsieur, Madame, Mademoiselle Surname,
Unnamed person	Dear Sir, Dear Madam,
Company/organisation	Dear Sirs,

Closing phrase:

to a named individual	Yours sincerely,
to a company/organisation or unnamed individual	Yours faithfully,

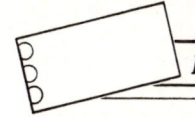

Notes on customs & practices

On the **envelope**, initials are used only when the forename is not known. The first forename only is usually written except where a forename is hyphenated. The visiting card is usually a good indicator of how the recipient likes to be addressed. Except at senior level, it is the normal practice to write to the department of the firm or organisation and not to an individual. In the **letter**, when writing in French the surname is usually omitted in the salutation.

SWITZERLAND

THE ENVELOPE

Addressed to the equivalent of:

Mr	Initials	Surname	Herrn Initials Surname
Mrs	"	"	Frau Initials Surname
Miss	"	"	Fräulein Initials Surname
Doctor	"	"	Herrn *or* Dr. Initials Surname
Engineer	"	"	Herrn *or* Frau Dipl.Ing. Initials Surname

Example of a typical address:

Name	Herrn Dr. Paul A. Meier
Position	Der Verkoufsleiter
Company	Bietenholz & Co AG
Street	Im Kehr 28
Town	CH–8330 PFAFFIKON
Country	Switzerland

THE LETTER If written in German

Opening salutation corresponding to:

Dear Mr	Surname	Sehr geehrter Herr Surname,
Dear Mrs	"	Sehr geehrte Frau Surname,
Dear Miss	"	Sehr geehrtes Fräulein Surname,
*Dear Doctor	"	Sehr geehrter Herr Doktor Surname,
*Dear Engineer	"	Sehr geehrter Herr Dipl.Ing. Surname,
Dear Sir		(*see note*)
Dear Sirs		Sehr geehrte Damen und Herren,

Substitute Frau for females and alter geehrter to geehrte.

Closing phrase:

to an individual	Mit freundlichen Grüssen
to a company/organisation	Hochachtungsvoll

(German speaking)

THE LETTER If written in English

Opening salutation to:

Mr	Dear Mr Surname, *or* Dear Herr Surname,
Mrs	Dear Mrs Surname, *or* Dear Frau Surname,
Miss	Dear Miss Surname, *or* Dear Fräulein Surname,
Doctor	Dear Dr Surname, *or* Dear Herr Dr. Surname,
Engineer	Dear Mr, Mrs, Miss Surname, *or* Dear Herr Dipl.Ing. Surname,
Un-named person	Dear Sir, *or* Madam, *or* (*see note*)
Company/organisation	Dear Sirs,

In the above examples both the Doctor and Engineer are treated as male. Substitute Frau for females.

Closing phrase:

to a named individual	Yours sincerely,
to a company/organisation	Yours faithfully,

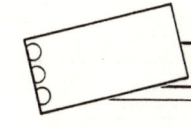

Notes on customs & practices

The envelope

The first forename may be used in substitution for the initial. The visiting card is usually a good indicator of how the recipient likes to be addressed. Position may be linked with name or written on a separate line. Except at senior level, it is normal practice to write to the department of the firm or organisation and not to an individual.

The letter

Whilst Dear Sir in English is acceptable, the German equivalent Sehr geehrter Herr is not polite. On coming of age unmarried women are addressed on the envelope and in the salutation as Frau and not Fräulein.

SWITZERLAND

THE ENVELOPE

Addressed to the equivalent of:

Mr	Initials	Surname	Egregio Signor Initials Surname *or* Egr.Sig. Initials Surname
Mrs	"	"	Gentile Signora Initials Surname *or* Gent.ma Sig.ra Initials Surname
Miss	"	"	Gentile Signorina Initials Surname *or* Gent.ma Sig.na Initials Surname
Doctor	"	"	Egregio Dottor Initials Surname *or* Egr.Dott. Initials Surname
Engineer	"	"	Egregio Ingegner Initials Surname *or* Egr.Ing. Initials Surname

The above assumes the Doctor and Engineer are both male. Write Gentile Dottoressa Initials Surname and Gentile Ingegner Initials Surname if female.

Example of a typical address:

Name	Egr.Sig. S L Palgimi
Position	Direttore
Company	Biochimica AG
Street	Via Aldo Stazione 67
Town	CH–834 LOCANO
Country	Switzerland

THE LETTER If written in Italian

Opening salutation corresponding to:

Dear Mr	Surname	Egregio Signor Surname,
Dear Mrs	"	Gentile Signora Surname,
Dear Miss	"	Gentile Signorina Surname,
*Dear Doctor	"	Egregio Dottor Surname,
*Dear Engineer	"	Egregio Ingegner Surname,
Dear Sir		Egregio Signore,
Dear Sirs		Egregio Signori,

*Write Gentile Dottoressa Surname and Gentile Ingegner Surname if female.

(Italian speaking)

Closing phrase:

to an individual — Distinti saluti, *or* La prego di gradire i miei piu cordiali saluti

to a company/organisation — Distinti saluti

THE LETTER If written in English

Opening salutation to:

Mr	Dear Mr Surname, *or* Dear Signor Surname,
Mrs	Dear Mrs Surname, *or* Dear Signora Surname,
Miss	Dear Miss Surname, *or* Dear Signorina Surname,
*Doctor	Dear Dr Surname, *or* Dear Dottor Surname,
Engineer	Dear Mr, Mrs, Miss Surname, *or* Dear Ingegner Surname,
Unnamed person	Dear Sir, *or* Madam,
Company/organisation	Dear Sirs,

Write Dear Dottoressa Surname if female.

Closing phrase:

to a named individual — Yours sincerely,

to a company/organisation or unnamed individual — Yours faithfully,

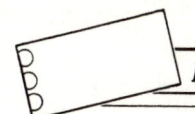

Notes on customs & practices

On the **envelope**, it is the custom to abbreviate the titles. The first forename may be used in place of an initial. The visiting card is usually a good indicator of how the recipient likes to be addressed. Except at senior level, it is normal practice to write to the department of the firm or organisation and not to an individual. In the **letter**, in the salutation Egregio Signore is sometimes omitted and Egregio Signori is often omitted.

TURKEY

THE ENVELOPE

Addressed to the equivalent of:

Mr	Initials	Surname	Bay Initials Surname
Mrs	"	"	Bayan Initials Surname
Miss	"	"	Bayan Initials Surname
Doctor	"	"	Doktor Initials Surname
Engineer	"	"	Yüksek Mühendis Initials Surname

Example of a typical address:

Name	Bay Ö Sakir
Position	Genel Müdür
Company	Artan Tibbi Müstakzarat Ltd S
Street	Kocabey Sokak No: 53
Town	Aksaray ISTANBUL
Country	Turkey

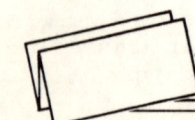

THE LETTER If written in Turkish

Opening salutation corresponding to:

Dear Mr	Surname	Sayin Forename Bey,
Dear Mrs	"	Sayin Forename Hanim,
Dear Miss	"	Sayin Forename Hanim,
Dear Doctor	"	Sayin Doktor Surname,
Dear Engineer	"	Sayin Y. Mühendis Surname,
Dear Sir, Dear Madam,		Sayin Bay, Sayin Bayan,
Dear Sirs		Sayin Bay or Sayin Beyefendi,

Closing phrase:

to an individual	Saygilarimla, (*with my kind regards*)
to a company/organisation	Saygilarimizla, (*with our kind regards*)

THE LETTER If written in English

Opening salutation to:

Mr	Dear Mr Surname, *or* Dear Forename Bey,
Mrs	Dear Mrs Surname, *or* Dear Forename Hanim,
Miss	Dear Miss Surname, *or* Dear Forename Hanim,
Doctor	Dear Dr Surname, *or* Dear Dr. Surname,
Engineer	Dear Mr, Mrs, Miss Surname, *or* Dear Y. Mühendis Surname,
Unnamed person	Dear Sir, Dear Madam,
Company/organisation	Dear Sirs,

Closing phrase:

to a named individual	Yours sincerely,
to a company/organisation or unnamed individual	Yours faithfully,

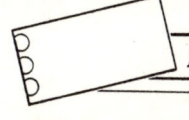

Notes on customs & practices

The envelope

It is usual to employ initials rather than the forenames but the visiting card is a good indicator of how the recipient likes to be addressed. It is common practice to write to individuals or to the department of the firm or organisation.

The letter

In the opening salutation the recipient is addressed by his or her forename and not the surname except in the cases where a professional title is used.

French is sometimes a preferred alternative to English if the writer does not use Turkish.

Business Letters to Eastern European Countries

ALBANIA

THE ENVELOPE

Addressed to the equivalent of:

Mr	Initials	Surname	Zoti Initials Surname
Mrs	"	"	Zonja Initials Surname
Miss	"	"	Zonjusha Initials Surname
Doctor	"	"	Doktori Initials Surname (*Male*)
			Doktoresha Initials Surname (*Female*)
Engineer	"	"	Inxhinieri Initials Surname (*Male*)
			Inxhinierja Initials Surname (*Female*)

Example of a typical address:

Name	Zoti Rahman Toska
Position	
Organisation	Makinaimport
Street	'Rruga 4 Shkurti'
Town	TIRANË
Country	Albania

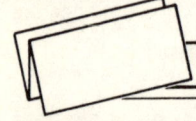

THE LETTER If written in Albanian

Opening salutation corresponding to:

Dear Mr	Surname	I dashur zoti Surname,
Dear Mrs	"	E dashur zonja Surname,
Dear Miss	"	E dashur zonjusha Surname,
Dear Doctor	"	I dashur doktori Surname,
Dear Engineer	"	I dashur inxhinieri Surname,

Dear Sir, Dear Madam,   I dashur zotëri, E dashur zonjë,
Dear Sirs   Të dashur zotërinj,

*In the above examples the Doctor and Engineer are male. If female write
E dashur doktoresha Surname and E dashur inxhinierja Surname.*

Closing phrase:

to an individual   Me përshëndetje miqësore,
to a company/organisation   Me nderime,

THE LETTER If written in Italian

Opening salutation to:

Mr   Egregio Signor Surname,
Mrs   Gentile Signora Surname,
Miss   Gentile Signorina Surname,
Doctor   Egregio Dottor Surname,
Engineer   Egregio Ingegner Surname,
Un-named person   Egregio Signore, (*or* Egregio Signora)
Company/organisation   Egregio Signori,

*The above assumes the Doctor and Engineer are both male. Write Gentile
Dottoressa Surname and Gentile Ingegner Surname if female.*

Closing phrase:

to a named individual   Distinti saluti
to a company/organisation or   Distinti saluti
unnamed individual

Notes on customs & practices

Foreign trade is controlled through the Ministry of Commerce by the appropriate State Trading Organisation. The practice is to write, regarding purchases from Albania, to the Albanian Embassy in Rome or the Albanian Embassy in Paris. The practice regarding sales to Albania is to write to the appropriate State Trading Organisation in Albania with copy correspondence to the Albanian Embassy in Rome.

The envelope

This may be addressed in Albanian as above in the example:

The letter

If not written in Albanian, this should preferably be in Italian or French as next choice. Russian is an alternative.

BULGARIA

THE ENVELOPE

Addressed to the equivalent of:

Mr	Initials	Surname	Г-н	Initials Surname
Mrs	"	"	Г-жа	Initials Surname
Miss	"	"	Г-ца	Initials Surname
Doctor	"	"	Д-р	Initials Surname
Engineer	"	"	Инж.	Initials Surname

Example of a typical address:

Country	Bulgaria
Town	SOFIVA 1517
Street	Konstantin Fotinov 2
Organisation	Targovsko Obzavezhdane
Name	B Chakarov

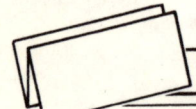

THE LETTER If written in Bulgarian

Opening salutation corresponding to:

(*Surname usually omitted, except with Doctor*)

Dear Mr	Surname	Уважаеми господине,
Dear Mrs	"	Уважаема госпожо,
Dear Miss	"	Уважаема госпожице,
Dear Doctor	"	Уважаеми Д-р Surname,
Dear Engineer	"	Уважаеми инж.
Dear Sir, Dear Madam		Уважаеми господине, уважаема госпожо,
Dear Sirs		Уважаеми господа,

Closing phrase:

to an individual	Искрено Ваш, or С поздрав, or С уважение,
to a company/organisation	С уважение,

72

THE LETTER If written in English

Opening salutation to:

Mr	Dear Mr Surname	
Mrs	Dear Mrs Surname	*If writing in English,*
Miss	Dear Miss Surname	*it is preferable to use*
Doctor	Dear Dr Surname	*the English salutations*
Engineer	Dear Mr, Mrs, Miss Surname	*opposite*
Unnamed person	Dear Sir, Dear Madam,	
Company/organisation	Dear Sirs,	

Closing phrase:

to a named individual	Yours sincerely,
to a company/organisation or unnamed individual	Yours faithfully,

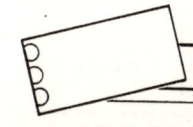

Notes on customs & practices

Foreign trade is conducted through the appropriate Foreign Trade Organisation and Enterprises dealing with foreign trade.

Correspondence, if not in Bulgarian, should be in English or Russian.

Western type for the address is usual practice even when the letter is in Bulgarian.

Commonly used translations are:

General Director: Генерален директор

Head of Foreign Relations Department: Директор на Дирекция "Международни връзки"

British Desk: Направление "Великобритания"

CZECHOSLOVAKIA

THE ENVELOPE

Addressed to the equivalent of:

Mr	Initials	Surname	Pan Initials Surname
Mrs	"	"	Paní Initials Surname
Miss	"	"	Slečna Initials Surname
Doctor	"	"	Pan Dr. Initials Surname
			or Paní or Slečna Initials Surname
Engineer	"	"	Pan Ing. Initials Surname
			or Paní or Slečna Initials Surname

Example of a typical address:

Name	Pan Jan Novák
Position	podnikový ředitel
Company	STROJOBAL n.p.
Street	Řeznická 8
Town	110 00 PRAHA 1
Country	Czechoslovakia

THE LETTER If written in Czech

Opening salutation corresponding to:

Dear Mr	Surname	Vážený pane Surname,
Dear Mrs	"	Vážená paní Surname,
Dear Miss	"	Vážená slečna Surname,
Dear Doctor	"	Vážený pane doktore Surname,
Dear Engineer	"	Vážený pane inženýre Surname,
Dear Sir, Dear Madam:		Vážený pane, Vážená paní,
Dear Sirs		Vážení pánové,

In the above examples the Doctor and Engineer are male. If female, substitute paní or slečna for pane.

Closing phrase:

to an individual	S pozdravem; Se srdečným pozdravem,
to a company/organisation	S pozdravem; Se srdečným pozdravem,

(Czech speaking)

THE LETTER If written in English

Opening salutation to:

Mr	Dear Mr Surname, *or* Dear pane Surname,	*Unusual to mix English with Czechoslovakian*
Mrs	Dear Mrs Surname, *or* Dear paní Surname,	
Miss	Dear Miss Surname Dear slečna Surname,	
Doctor	Dear Dr Surname,	
Engineer	Dear Mr, Mrs, Miss Surname,	
Un-named person	Dear Sir, or Dear Madam,	
Company/organisation	Dear Sirs,	

Closing phrase:

to a named individual	Yours sincerely,
to a company/organisation or unnamed individual	Yours faithfully,

Notes on customs & practices

Most business letters are addressed to the Federal Ministry of Foreign Trade or to Foreign Trade Organisations. If letters are not written in Czech or Slovak, French or Spanish is understood but German and English are better. Examples are shown below of common forms of address used. Where alternatives are given, selection depends upon the organisation to which the letter is written.

It is usual practice to address letters to a department with a salutation corresponding to Dear Sirs or Dear Mr General Director as appropriate.

In writing private letters, it is preferable to use the forename, if known, rather than initials.

Common terms used when writing to Federal Ministry of Foreign Trade or Foreign Trade Organisations: General Director – generální ředitel: Head of Foreign Relations Department – vedoucí mezinárodního oddělen *or* vedoucí odboru mezinárodních vztahů: British Desk – britské oddělení or britský referát or britský odbor.

CZECHOSLOVAKIA

THE ENVELOPE

Addressed to the equivalent of:

Mr	Initials	Surname	Pán Initials Surname
Mrs	"	"	Paní Initials Surname
Miss	"	"	Slečna Initials Surname
Doctor	"	"	Pán Dr. Initials Surname
			or Paní or Slečna Initials Surname
Engineer	"	"	Pán Ing. Initials Surname or Paní or Slečna

Example of a typical address:

Name	Pán
	Ján Novák
Position	podnikový riaditeI
Company	LIKO n.p.
Street	Dunajská 12
Town	800 00 BRATISLAVA
Country	Czechoslovakia

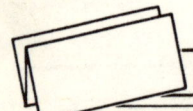

THE LETTER If written in Slovak

Opening salutation corresponding to:

Dear Mr	Surname	Vážený pán Surname,
Dear Mrs	"	Vážená paní Surname,
Dear Miss	"	Vážená slečna Surname,
Dear Doctor	"	Vážený pan doktor Surname,
Dear Engineer	"	Vážený pán inžinier Surname,
Dear Sir Dear Madam:		Vážený pán, Vážená paní,
Dear Sirs		Vážení páni,

In the above examples the Doctor and Engineer are male. If female, substitute paní or slečna for pán.

Closing phrase:

to an individual	S pozdravom,
	So srdečným pozdravom,
to a company/organisation	S pozdravom,
	So srdečným pozdravom,

(Slovak speaking)

THE LETTER If written in English

Opening salutation to:

Mr	Dear Mr Surname, *or* Dear pán Surname,	*Unusual to mix English with Slovakian*
Mrs	Dear Mrs Surname, *or* Dear paní Surname,	
Miss	Dear Miss Surname *or* Dear slečna Surname,	
Doctor	Dear Dr Surname,	
Engineer	Dear Mr, Mrs, Miss Surname,	
Unnamed person	Dear Sir, or Dear Madam,	
Company/organisation	Dear Sirs,	

Closing phrase:

to a named individual	Yours sincerely,
to a company/organisation or unnamed individual	Yours faithfully,

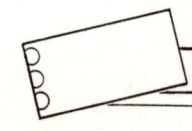

Notes on customs & practices

Most business letters are addressed to the Federal Ministry of Foreign Trade or to Foreign Trade Organisations. If letters are not written in Czech or Slovak, French or Spanish is understood but German and English are better. Examples are shown below of common forms of address used. Where alternatives are given, selection depends upon the organisation to which the letter is written. It is usual practice to address letters to a department with a salutation corresponding to Dear Sirs or Dear Mr General Director as appropriate. In writing private letters it is preferable to use the forename, if known, rather than initials.

Common terms used when writing to Federal Ministry of Foreign Trade or Foreign Trade Organisations: General Director – generálny riaditeI: Head of Foreign Relations Department – vedúci medzinárodného oddelenia *or* vedúci odboru medzinárodných vzťahov: British Desk-britské oddelenie *or* britský referát

EAST GERMANY

THE ENVELOPE

Addressed to the equivalent of:

Mr	Initials	Surname	Herrn Initials Surname
Mrs	"	"	Frau Initials Surname
Miss	"	"	Fräulein Initials Surname
Doctor	"	"	Herrn *or* Frau Dr Initials Surname
Engineer	"	"	Herrn *or* Frau Initials Surname

Example of a typical address:

Organisation	VEB Jenapharm
Position	Direktor
Name	Herrn H Herrmann
Street	Dohnaer Strasse 103
Town	DDR – 6900 JENA
Country	German Democratic Republic

THE LETTER If written in German

Opening salutation corresponding to:

Dear Mr	Surname	Sehr geehrter Herr Surname!
Dear Mrs	"	Sehr geehrte Frau Surname!
Dear Miss	"	Sehr geehrtes Fräulein Surname!
Dear Doctor	"	Sehr geehrter Herr Dr. Surname!
Dear Engineer	"	Sehr geehrter Herr Surname!
Dear Sir, or Madam,		(*see notes*)
Dear Sirs		Sehr geehrte Damen und Herren! *or if male only*, Sehr geehrte Herren!

For female Doctor substitute geehrte Frau. For female Engineer, substitute geehrte Frau.

Closing phrase:

to an individual	Hochachtungsvoll
to a company/organisation	"

(German Democratic Republic)

THE LETTER If written in English

Opening salutation to:

Mr	Dear Mr Surname, *or* Dear Herr Surname,
Mrs	Dear Mrs Surname, *or* Dear Frau Surname,
Miss	Dear Miss Surname, *or* Dear Fräulein Surname,
*Doctor	Dear Dr Surname, *or* Dear Herr Dr. Surname,
Engineer	Dear Mr, Mrs, Miss Surname,
Unnamed person	Dear Sir, *or* Madam,
Company/organisation	Dear Sirs,

Substitute Frau for females.

Closing phrase:

to a named individual	Yours sincerely,
to a company/organisation or unnamed individual	Yours faithfully,

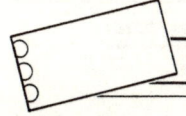

Notes on customs & practices

The envelope

Most business letters will be addressed to a Foreign Trade Enterprise probably located in Berlin. It is usual to write to a named person once preliminaries have been completed. Often State Agency Companies need to be appointed as representatives. Note the layout of the address which differs from Western practice.

The letter

Correspondence is more effective if in German. English, whilst acceptable, is very much second choice. Dear Sir or Dear Madam in German is not polite. If possible use the person's name. It is the practice to address unmarried mature women as Frau.

The titles General Director, Head of Foreign Relations Department and British Desk are translated into– Generaldirektor, Leiter der handelspolitischen Abteilung, and, Länderabteilung Großbritannien.

HUNGARY

THE ENVELOPE

Addressed to the equivalent of:

Mr	Initials	Surname	Surname Forename
Mrs	"	"	Surname Forename
Miss	"	"	Surname Forename
Doctor	"	"	Doktor Surname Forename
			or Dr. Surname Forename
Engineer	"	"	Surname Forename mérnök

Example of a typical address:

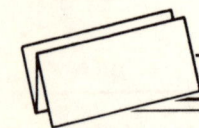

Name	Kozma Miklós
Position	Vezérigazgató
Organisation	NIKEX
Town	BUDAPEST
Street/Road	Meszáros u. 48/54.
Postcode	H – 1016
Country	Hungary

THE LETTER If written in Hungarian

Opening salutation corresponding to:

Dear Mr	Surname	Tisztelt Surname úr!
Dear Mrs	"	Tisztelt Surnamené! (like: Kozmáné)*
Dear Miss	"	Tisztelt Surname kisasszony!
Dear Doctor	"	Tisztelt Surname doktor úr!
Dear Engineer	"	Tisztelt Surname mérnök úr!
Dear Sir,		Tisztelt uram!
Dear Sirs,		Tisztelt uraim!
Dear Madam,		Tisztelt asszonyom!

The practice of adding 'né' to the husband's surname does not always follow and if not sure, it is safer to open with 'Tisztelt asszonyom'

Closing phrase:

to an individual } Tisztelettel: *or*
to a company/organisation } Kiváló tisztelettel:

THE LETTER If written in English

Opening salutation to:

Mr	Dear Mr Surname, *or*
	Dear Surname úr!
Mrs	Dear Mrs Surname, *or*
	Dear Madam,
Miss	Dear Miss Surname, *or*
	Dear Surname kisasszony!
Doctor	Dear Dr Surname,
Engineer	Dear Mr, Mrs, Miss Surname,
Unnamed person	Dear Sir, Dear Madam,
Company/organisation	Dear Sirs,

Closing phrase:

to a named individual	Yours sincerely,
to a company/organisation or unnamed individual	Yours faithfully,

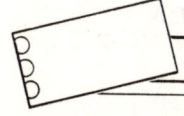

Notes on customs & practices

Foreign trade is conducted through State-owned Agencies or Companies entrusted with foreign trade rights. Letters if not written in Hungarian should be either in German or in English. Envelopes may be addressed to departments, individuals or both, with the appropriate salutation in the letter. The following translations apply frequently in letters to State-owned Agencies:

General Director – Vezérigazgató (Dear General Director, = Tisztelt Vezérigazgató úr!) Head of Foreign Relations Department – Nemzetközi Kapcsolatok Főosztályvezetöje (Opening salutation = Tisztelt Főosztályvezető úr!) British Desk – Brit előadó (Opening salutation = Tisztelt Surname úr!)

POLAND

THE ENVELOPE

Addressed to the equivalent of:

Mr	Initials	Surname	Pan Initials Surname
Mrs	"	"	Pani Initials Surname
Miss	"	"	Pani Initials Surname
Doctor	"	"	Dr Initials Surname
Engineer	"	"	Inż. Initials Surname

Example of a typical address:

Name	Dyrektor A Kowalski
Position	
Company	AGROS
Street	ul Chalubinskiego 8
Town	WARSZAWA
Country	Poland

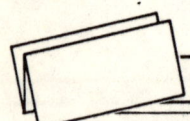

THE LETTER If written in Polish

Opening salutation corresponding to:

Dear Mr	Surname	Szanowny Panie,
Dear Mrs	"	Szanowna Pani,
Dear Miss	"	Szanowna Pani,
Dear Doctor	"	Szanowny Panie Doktorze,
Dear Engineer	"	Szanowny Panie Inżynierze,
Dear Sir, Dear Madam,		Szanowny Panie, Szanowna Pani,
Dear Sirs		Szanowni Państwo,

Closing phrase:

to an individual
to a company/organisation } Z poważaniem,

THE LETTER If written in English

Opening salutation to:

Mr	Dear Mr Surname,	
Mrs	Dear Mrs Surname,	
Miss	Dear Miss Surname,	*It is not usual to*
Doctor	Dear Dr Surname,	*combine the*
Engineer	Dear Mr, Mrs, Miss Surname,	*English 'Dear' with the Polish*
Unnamed person	Dear Sir, Dear Madam,	*'Mr' etc.*
Company/organisation	Dear Sirs,	

Closing phrase:

to a named individual	Yours sincerely,
to a company/organisation or unnamed individual	Yours faithfully,

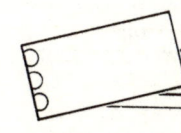

Notes on customs & practices

Foreign trade is conducted through the appropriate state Foreign Trade Enterprise and companies and individuals licensed by the Minister of Foreign Trade. The translations of General Director, Head of Foreign Relations Department and British Desk are: Dyrektor Generalny, Dyrektor Departamentu or Kierownik Wydziału, Wydział Brytyjski.

The envelope

Always address the individual by name if known. The business or professional titles should be used. The visiting card is usually a good indicator of how the individual likes to be addressed.

The letter

The professional title is usually included in the salutation.

ROMANIA

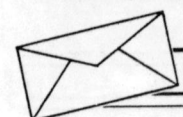

THE ENVELOPE

Addressed to the equivalent of:

Mr	Initials	Surname	D-lui Initials Surname
Mrs	"	"	D-nei Initials Surname
Miss	"	"	D-soarei Initials Surname
Doctor	"	"	D-lui Doctor Surname
Engineer	"	"	D-lui Inginer Surname

Example of a typical address:

Name	D-lui P Golescu
Organisation	Danubiana
Town	BUCURESTI
Street	202A Splaiul Indpendentei
Country	Romania

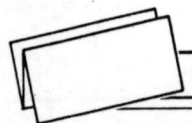

THE LETTER If written in Romanian

Opening salutation corresponding to:

Dear Mr	Surname	Stimate domnule Surname,
Dear Mrs	"	Stimata doamna Surname,
Dear Miss	"	Stimată domnişoară Surname
Dear Doctor	"	Stimate domnule Doctor Surname,
Dear Engineer	"	Stimate domnule Inginer Surname,
Dear Sir, Dear Madam,		Stimate Domn, Stimata Doamna,
Dear Sirs Dear Madams		Stimaţi domni, stimate doamne,

Closing phrase:

to an individual	cu stima,
to a company/organisation	cu deosebită stimă,

THE LETTER If written in English

Opening salutation to:

Mr	Dear Mr Surname,	*If writing in English*
Mrs	Dear Mrs Surname,	*it is preferred that*
Miss	Dear Miss Surname,	*the title is wholly in English also.*

Doctor	Dear Dr Surname,
Engineer	Dear Mr, Mrs, Miss Surname,
Unnamed person	Dear Sir, Dear Madam,
Company/organisation	Dear Sirs,

Closing phrase:

to a named individual	Yours sincerely,
to a company/organisation or unnamed individual	Yours faithfully,

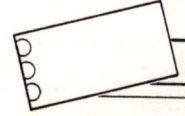

Notes on customs & practices

Foreign trade is conducted through the appropriate Foreign Trade Enterprise. Business letters if not written in Romanian should be French, German or English. Envelopes may be addressed to departments, individuals or both with the appropriate salutation in the letter. The following translations apply frequently in letters to State organisations:

The envelope

to the General Director, D-lui Director General

The letter

Opening salutation – Stimate domnule Director General; Head of Foreign Relations Department translates to Seful Biroului Protocol and The British Desk into Relatia Anglia *or* Marea Britanie.

USSR

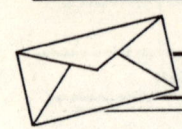

THE ENVELOPE

Addressed to the equivalent of:

Mr	Initials	Surname	Господин	Initials Surname
Mrs	"	"	Госпожа	Initials Surname
Miss	"	"	Госпожа	Initials Surname
Doctor	"	"	Доктор	Initials Surname
Engineer	"	"	Инженер	Initials Surname
General Director			Генеральный Директор	

Example of a typical address:

Town	MOSKVA Zh – 17
Street	Pyatnitskaya Ulitsa
Number	50/2
Organisation	V/O Avtopromimport
Name	A A Butko
Country	USSR

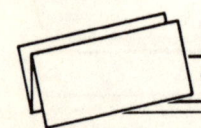

THE LETTER If written in Russian

Opening salutation corresponding to:

Dear Mr	Surname	Уважаемый Господин,	
Dear Mrs	"	Уважаемая Госпожа,	
Dear Miss	"	Уважаемая Госпожа,	"
Dear Doctor	"	Уважаемый Господин,	
Dear Engineer	"	Уважаемый Господин,	"
Dear Sir		Уважаемый Господин,	"
Dear Sirs		Уважаемые Господа,	
Dear General Director		Уважаемый Господин Генеральный Директор,	
Dear Minister		Уважаемый Министр,	

Closing phrase:

to an individual
to a company/organisation } С уважением,

THE LETTER If written in English

Opening salutation to:

Mr	Dear Mr Surname,	
Mrs	Dear Mrs Surname,	*The opening*
Miss	Dear Miss Surname,	*salutation should be*
Doctor	Dear Dr Surname,	*all in English or all*
Engineer	Dear Mr, Mrs, Miss Surname,	*in Russian. Any combination is to be*
Unnamed person	Dear Sir, Dear Madam	*avoided.*
Company/organisation	Dear Sirs,	

Closing phrase:

to a named individual — Yours sincerely,
to a company/organisation or unnamed individual — Yours faithfully,

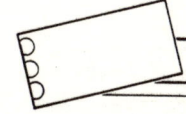

Notes on customs & practices

Foreign trade is conducted through the appropriate Foreign Trade Organisation. Business letters are so addressed and/or to the Foreign Relations Department of a Ministry.

The envelope

Roman type is usual even if the letter itself is in Russian (if sent from outside Russia). Initials are used in preference to forename(s). If written in Roman type the title of Mr, Mrs etc, is usually omitted.

The letter

To have greatest impact this should be written in Russian. In the salutation Miss is the same as Mrs, and a Doctor, Engineer and a Mr are all treated as Dear Sir.

British Desk is translated as   Британский Отдел
Head of Foreign Relations Department as   Начальник Управления внешних отношений

YUGOSLAVIA

THE ENVELOPE

Addressed to the equivalent of:

Mr	Initials	Surname	Drug Forename Surname
Mrs	"	"	Drugarica Forename Surname
Miss	"	"	Drugarica Forename Surname
Doctor	"	"	Dr. Forename Surname
Engineer	"	"	Forename Surname, Dipl.Ing.

Example of a typical address:

Name	Drug Petar Petrović
Position	Direktor
Organisation	Generalexport
Street	Narodnih Heroja 59
Town	11000 BEOGRAD
Country	Yugoslavia

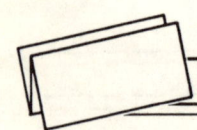

THE LETTER If written in Serbo-Croat

Opening salutation corresponding to:

Dear Mr	Surname	Poštovani Druže Surname,
Dear Mrs	"	Poštovana Drugarica Surname,
Dear Miss	"	Poštovana Drugarica Surname,
Dear Doctor	"	Poštovani Doutore Surname,
Dear Engineer	"	Poštovani Inžinjeru Surname,
Dear Sir, Dear Madam,		Poštovani Druže, Poštovana Drugarice,
Dear Sirs		Poštovani Drugovi,

The ending to the surname changes in Serbo-Croat and in the example of Petrović the letter u is added in the case of the salutation to a Mr and an engineer.

Closing phrase:

to an individual
to a company/organisation } Drugarski Pozdrav,

THE LETTER If written in English

Opening salutation to:

Mr	Dear Mr Surname,	*It is not acceptable in*
Mrs	Dear Mrs Surname,	*Yugoslavia to write,*
Miss	Dear Miss Surname,	*for example, Dear*
Doctor	Dear Dr Surname,	*Druže Surname, one*
Engineer	Dear Mr, Mrs, Miss Surname,	*writes either in English throughout or*
Unnamed person	Dear Sir, Dear Madam	*in Serbo-Croat.*
Company/organisation	Dear Sirs,	

Closing phrase:

to a named individual	Yours sincerely,
to a company/organisation or unnamed individual	Yours faithfully,

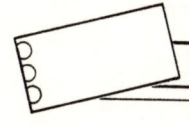

Notes on customs & practices

Foreign trade is usually conducted through Enterprises registered for import/export or manufacturers registered for foreign trade. If Serbo-Croat is not used in writing, English or German will probably be understood.

If writing privately as opposed to a company, on the envelope substitute Gospodin, Gospodja and Gospodica for Drug, Drugarica and Drugarica. In the salutation substitute Gospodine, Gospodo and Gospodice for Druže, Drugarica and Drugarica.

GUIDELINES FOR LETTERS TO VARIOUS IMPORTANT TRADING NATIONS

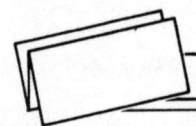

ARAB RECIPIENTS

English (or French where indicated) is usually understood commercially and may be used, observing the conventions noted below. Letters to Government Agencies and all trade literature should, however, be in Arabic.

English can be used commercially in the following countries:

Bahrain	Lebanon	South Yemen
Egypt	Libya[b]	Sudan
Ethiopia[a]	Oman	Syria
Iraq	Qatar	United Arab Emirates
Jordon	Saudi Arabia	Yemen Arab Republic
Kuwait	Somalia[a]	

French can be used commercially in:

Algeria	Mauritania
Chad	Morocco
Comoros	Tunisia
Djibouti[a]	

Notes (1)

[a] Not strictly Arab countries but Arabic is spoken and widely understood.
[b] If not known to the recipient, it is better to use Arabic, at least initially.

In the instructions given below it is assumed in all cases that the recipient is male. If in doubt as to which name to use in the salutation, then use Dear Sir.

The envelope

In English or French address to Sayyed all names (do not use initials)

The letter – opening salutation

In English:

Dear Sayyed Final Name except where Abu or Abdel preceeds it, in which case write

Dear Sayyed Abu/Abdel Final Name

Except use the first name in Sudan, Saudi Arabia, Oman and United Arab Emirates.

In French:

As above except use Cher in place of Dear

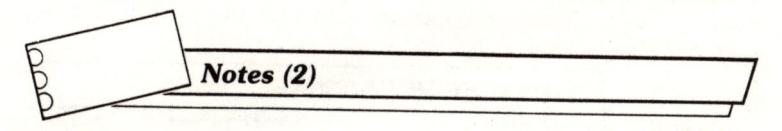

Notes (2)

In Gulf States and Saudi Arabia the recipient in business may be a Sheikh in which case Sheikh is used in place of Sayyed.

In Kuwait, Government Ministers, President of the Chamber of Commerce and local people of importance are addressed as Your Excellency.

In Egypt it is sometimes preferable to begin the salutation and address the envelope using Mr in place of Sayyed.

CHINESE RECIPIENTS

Commercial letters are acceptable in English.

Trade is usually conducted through State Trading Corporations which are controlled by the Ministry of Foreign Economic Relations and Trade.

The envelope

An example in English is:

> China National Technical Import Corporation
> Erligou
> Xijiao
> Beijing
> The People's Republic of China

Where the name of the recipient is known:

> Mr all names

or

> Mme all names

The letter

Dear Mr first name (*ie the family name*)
or
Dear Mme first name

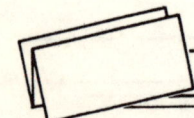

JAPANESE RECIPIENTS

Commercial letters are acceptable in English.

The envelope } Follow the English
The letter } conventions.

MALAYSIA, SINGAPORE & BRUNEI RECIPIENTS

Commercial letters written in English:

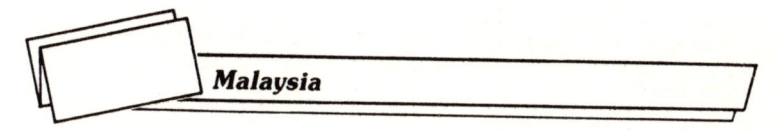

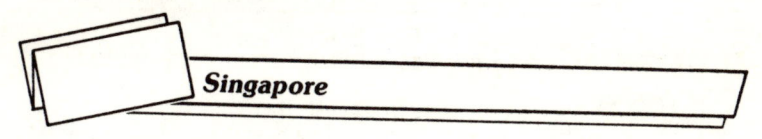

Malaysia

The envelope

Addressed to a Malay:
  (Mr) Encik all names
  (Mrs) Puan all names
  (Miss) Cik all names
Addressed to a Chinese or Indian:
  Mr all names
  Mrs all names
  Miss all names

The letter

Addressed to a Malay:
```
           Encik
  Dear    Puan  first of names
           Cik
```
Addressed to a Chinese or Indian
```
           Mr
  Dear    Mrs  first of names
           Miss
```

Singapore

The envelope

Addressed to a Chinese or Indian
```
   Mr
   Mrs  all names
   Miss
```

The letter

```
           Mr
  Dear    Mrs  first of names
           Miss
```

Brunei

The envelope

Addressed to a male without a title:
 (Mr) Awang all names

The letter

 (Mr) Dear Awang first of names

BURMESE RECIPIENTS

Commercial letters are acceptable in English.

The envelope

To a Mr	U all names
To a Mrs or Miss	Daw all names

The letter

To a Mr	Dear U all names
To a Mrs or Miss	Dear Daw all names

THAI RECIPIENTS

Commercial letters are acceptable in English.

The envelope

To a Mr, Mrs, Miss	Khun all names

The letter

To a Mr, Mrs, Miss	Dear Khun first name